The Long Distance Millionaire

The Step-By-Step Process to Become a Millionaire Through Real Estate and Tenants

Andre Green

Print ISBN
979-8-9899174-0-2

eBook ISBN
979-8-9899174-1-9

Library of Congress Control Number
2024903838

First edition 2024.

Table of Contents

Chapter One: Mindset

Real estate is a lucrative industry that has attracted many people with the promise of financial stability and passive income. One of the most popular avenues in real estate is becoming a landlord, which involves renting out property to tenants. However, before getting into the landlord side of real estate, it is essential to shift your mindset from a renter to a business owner.

I've been in real estate for quite some time now, and I know that there are generally three types of landlords with three distinct personalities.

The Control Freak

If you're the type of person who desires complete control over every aspect of a project or process, then this book is tailored for you. However, as a long-distance landlord, it's important to recognize that you won't have absolute control over the entire real estate ownership and management process. Dealing with unpredictable tenants, uncontrollable contractors, and the unknowns can be challenging. As a landlord, you'll discover that each day brings unique situations, making it difficult to plan ahead. Nevertheless, you can still be prepared by equipping yourself with the knowledge and insights provided in this book.

The Laid-back Person

If you're someone who isn't overly concerned with the small details and is primarily focused on achieving the end result, this book acknowledges your emotional ease as a landlord. However, it emphasizes the importance of understanding every role in the real estate business to avoid losing control over your investment property. This book serves as your cheat sheet, providing essential knowledge that enables you to delegate effectively and operate a successful long-distance landlord business.

The Owner/Operator

As the "Mr. Know-it-All" type of person, you possess the ability to be hands-on when necessary but also understand the value of stepping back and letting others take charge. While you may feel uncertain about the initial steps, you have confidence in your ability to figure things out independently. However, it's crucial to be cautious as your confidence can lead to hasty actions that jeopardize your investment. This book is especially valuable to you as it offers a comprehensive framework and guidance, empowering you to make informed decisions and avoid potential pitfalls along the way.

Looping back to the title of the chapter, shifting your mindset means changing the way you think about things. When it comes to being a landlord, this means moving away from the mindset of a renter or homeowner and adopting a business-oriented mindset. Being a landlord is a business, and to be successful, you need to treat it as such. This includes having a clear understanding of your goals, finances, and responsibilities.

Before going into real estate, people may have a variety of mindset characteristics that influence their approach to the industry. Here are some common characteristics, and if you fit into some of these categories, it's okay; I have ways that you can overcome them to be the best long distance landlord (and millionaire) possible. Let's get started!

Fixed Mindset vs. Growth Mindset

A fixed mindset is the belief that your abilities and qualities are fixed and cannot be changed or improved upon. A good example of this is a very popular saying among middle-aged folks:

"You can't teach an old dog new tricks."

People with a fixed mindset believe that their talents, intelligence, and personality traits are set in stone, and they just are who they are. This mindset can be limiting and can prevent you from reaching your full potential. Above all else, it's simply untrue.

For example, let's look at an average, everyday guy named Mike. He wants to get into become a long distance landlord, but he believes that he isn't good at math and can't develop his mathematical abilities. As a result, Mike avoids opportunities that involve math, such as pursuing a career in finance or accounting, or taking on a real estate investment that involves complex financial calculations.

This is extremely detrimental to Mike's success because he really wants to increase his income so that he can quit his dead-end job and become his own boss.

In reality, real estate investing requires a commitment to continuous learning, adaptation, and problem-solving... something that Mike hasn't quite figured out for himself yet. People with a fixed mindset, like Mike, may struggle to adapt to changing market conditions, take calculated risks, or learn from their mistakes, but that doesn't mean that it's the end of the world; it just means that the approach has to be changed so that they can see things from a different perspective.

On the other hand, people with a growth mindset believe that their abilities and qualities can be developed through hard work, dedication, and learning. They see challenges as opportunities to learn and grow, rather than insurmountable obstacles. Individuals with a growth mindset believe that their abilities can be developed through dedication and hard work, and that intelligence and talent are not fixed traits. This is what separates the dreamers from the doers.

Let's go back to our example above. Instead of accepting the idea that he just isn't a math person, let's imagine that Mike has a growth mindset. Instead of accepting defeat, he would take his fate into his own hands by take quizzes to see what his learning style is. He would take classes or workshops about budgeting, taxes, or investments. Mike may even download some apps or join a local math group.

The difference between a fixed mindset and a growth mindset is literally going from "I can't do this thing and here's why" to "I can't do this thing yet, but I can start with this one small step."

Developing a growth mindset can be challenging, as it requires a willingness to step outside of one's comfort zone and embrace uncertainty. However, if you can relate to Mike and also struggle with a growth mindset, here are a few tips to overcome it:

- *Embrace challenges:* Rather than avoiding challenges, individuals with a growth mindset see them as opportunities for growth and development. Be willing to take on new challenges, even if you feel uncomfortable or unsure of yourself.

- *Embrace failure:* Failure is viewed as a natural part of the learning process, and individuals with a growth mindset do not let setbacks discourage them. Embrace failure as an opportunity to learn, reflect, and improve.

- *Embrace the learning process:* Individuals with a growth mindset focus on the journey of learning and development, rather than just the end result. You must come to understand that growth and improvement require dedication, hard work, and a willingness to learn from others.

- *Embrace effort:* Individuals with a growth mindset believe that effort is essential for success. Intelligence and talent are not fixed traits; they can be developed through dedication and hard work.

Fear of Failure vs. Resilience

Fear of failure is a type of anxiety that comes from the possibility of experiencing a negative outcome or failing to meet a particular goal. People who have a fear of failure tend to avoid taking risks or trying new things, for fear of not succeeding or being judged negatively by others. This fear can be particularly debilitating in the context of real estate investing, where taking risks and making difficult decisions is essential. To be specific, someone with a fear of failure may avoid investing in a property (even though they know it may be a good investment opportunity) for fear of losing money or making a mistake. They may also hesitate to make decisions, such as setting rental rates or deciding when to sell a property, for fear of making the wrong choice. When it comes to real estate, the fear of failure will make you fail fast.

"The fear of failure will make you fail fast."

This isn't to say that the fear of failure is illegitimate; it can definitely stem from a variety of sources, including past failures, self-doubt, and social pressure. It could be a result of childhood trauma and consistently being told that you aren't good enough. It could be a defense mechanism like perfectionism where you're overly critical of yourself. It could even be as simple as not knowing whether your goals will work out in your favor. All of these are valid experiences, and fear of failure can be particularly challenging to overcome, as it often involves facing one's fears and stepping outside of one's comfort zone.

However, it is important to overcome the fear of failure to achieve success in real estate investing. Taking calculated risks and making difficult decisions are an integral part of the real estate industry, and if you allow fear to hold you back, how could you possibly expect to be a long distance landlord who makes millions? Developing confidence in your abilities, setting realistic goals, and learning from failures can help you achieve success in real estate investing, and here's exactly how you can overcome some of that fear-mongering: by being resilient.

Resilience is the ability to adapt and bounce back from adversity, challenges, and setbacks — individuals who are resilient are able to maintain a positive attitude and persevere through difficult times, rather than being discouraged or overwhelmed by setbacks often see the most success. Look at real estate millionaires like Roy "Don" Peebles, Biddy Mason, Phillip Payton, Jr., Kyara Gray, and, well, me.

When you're resilient, you are able to cope with stress and adversity in healthy ways, such as seeking support from friends and family, practicing self-care, and developing problem-solving skills. You are able to learn from your mistakes and setbacks, rather than being defeated by them. As hard to hear as this may be, resilience is essential for dealing with unexpected challenges, such as a tenant defaulting on rent, unexpected property damage, or market downturns, so resilient investors are able to adapt to changing circumstances, identify new opportunities, and stay focused on their long-term goals.

If you resilience isn't your strength yet, and you're consistently paralyzed by the fear of failure, again, you will fail fast. Because we just talked about the importance of a growth mindset, I know that you're open to bettering yourself. Here is a recap of several strategies that you can use to build your resilience:

- *Focus on the positive:* Resilient individuals are able to maintain a positive attitude, even in the face of adversity. By focusing on the positive aspects of a situation, such as opportunities for learning and growth, you can maintain a resilient mindset.

- *Practice self-care:* Taking care of yourself physically and emotionally is essential for building resilience. This includes getting enough sleep, eating well, exercising regularly, and engaging in stress-reducing activities, such as meditation or yoga.

- *Seek support:* Building a strong support network of friends, family, and colleagues can help you cope with stress and adversity. Seeking out professional support, such as counseling or coaching, can also be helpful.

- *Develop problem-solving skills:* Resilient individuals are able to identify and solve problems effectively. Developing problem-solving skills, such as brainstorming, decision-making, and critical thinking, can help you become more resilient in the face of challenges.

Short-Term Thinking vs. Risk Tolerance

Let's say a woman named Shakirah suddenly inherits a single-family home. Over the course of a few days, she immediately decides to flip it to rent out within the next three months. She has a husband and two daughters, so she wants to quickly multiply her income to alleviate her family's financial stress by paying down school tuition, student loans, credit cards, and, of course, their current mortgage. Shakirah already can see how beneficial this could be, and she wants to start ASAP. She is thinking the same thing that most people who have families would think — she wants to take something positive and spin it into something that not only benefits her, but benefits her entire household for years to come. This is a noble gesture, right? On the surface, this is definitely something that should be commended. However, this yearn for immediate gratification is not good for her goals in the long run.

Short-term thinking refers to a mindset where you prioritize immediate benefits or gains over long-term success or outcomes. People who have a short-term thinking mindset tend to focus on short-term goals, such as making quick profits, rather than considering the potential long-term consequences of their actions.

A good example of this would be Shakirah, a new investor and potential landlord who decided to rent a property too quickly without doing her due diligence in vetting renters. Every few months she has to get the property manager to fix the plumbing, patch a wall, or address noise complaints. In a rush to get passive income quickly, she cut corners on property maintenance or improvements to save money in the short term, so costs keep piling up. What started off as something that should have been powering up her income is now burning through expenses.

In Shakirah's case, short-term thinking will eventually be detrimental to success in the real estate industry. Real estate investing is a long-term game that requires patience, strategic planning, and a willingness to delay gratification for the sake of long-term success. Focusing solely on short-term gains can lead to poor decision-making, missed opportunities, and long-term financial losses.

To overcome short-term thinking, it is important to prioritize long-term goals and consider the potential long-term consequences of actions. Investors should take the time to thoroughly research potential investments, carefully consider the potential risks and rewards, and develop a long-term strategy for each investment. By taking a more holistic, long-term approach to real estate investing, you can increase your chances of success and achieve your financial goals.

Now, let's imagine that Shakirah took a few weeks to think her plan through. Instead of rushing to make a decision, she practices what is referred to as risk tolerance. Risk tolerance is the degree of risk that an individual is willing to take on in pursuit of their goals or objectives. Her goal is to be able to create a lucrative means of passive income to free her family financially — not just for the short-term, but for as long as possible.

For potential landlords like you, developing a higher risk tolerance can help take advantage of opportunities that may offer greater returns, but also involve more risk. Here are some examples of what Shakirah, and you, could do to develop risk tolerance:

- *Educate themselves:* Knowledge is power, and the more you understand about the real estate market and the risks involved in investing, the more confident you'll feel in making decisions. Educate yourself on topics such as property valuation, financing options, and market trends, and the risks associated with each.

- *Start small:* Starting with smaller investments can help you gain experience and build confidence. Invest in a single property or a small portfolio of properties, and gradually increase your investments over time.

- *Diversify investments:* Diversification is a strategy for spreading risk across different investments. By diversifying investments, you can reduce your exposure to any one property or market, and minimize the impact of any one loss.

- *Seek advice from experts:* Seeking advice from experienced real estate professionals can help you make informed decisions and reduce their risk. Consult with real estate agents, property managers, and financial advisors to get advice on market trends, investment strategies, and risk management.

- *Be patient:* Real estate investing requires patience and a long-term perspective. Be prepared to hold onto your investments for several years or even decades, and don't be discouraged by short-term fluctuations in the market.

Lack of Financial Education vs. Financial Literacy

This topic is going to make a lot of readers uncomfortable, but again, we're approaching this from a growth mindset. Many of the clients whom I've mentored began with a serious lack of financial education. Most of it was due to lack of formal financial education, some of it was due to cultural attitudes toward money, and a good portion of it almost always included financial misinformation. Regardless of their reasons, they were able to move past those obstacles and become landlords of multiple properties in a short amount of time. If this is something that you struggle with, too, then you are able to be just as successful as they are and this is just the next step toward financial freedom.

A lack of financial education is a situation where an individual lacks the knowledge and skills needed to make informed financial decisions. People who have a lack of financial education may struggle to manage their finances, invest their money effectively, and plan for their financial future. As I mentioned several times before, real estate investing requires a solid understanding of financial concepts such as cash flow, return on investment, tax implications, and property valuation. Without this knowledge, you may struggle to make informed decisions, assess investment risks, and avoid financial missteps.

Financial education is the manifestation of a willingness to learn new skills and overcome one's financial biases and beliefs. Developing a solid understanding of financial concepts, learning from experienced investors, and seeking out financial advice can help you make informed decisions and avoid costly mistakes. Taking the time to develop a long-term financial plan can help you achieve your financial goals and secure your financial future. (I explain the SBS Academy, an experiential resource, in-depth throughout chapter thirteen.)

Investors with a high level of financial literacy are able to evaluate potential investment opportunities based on their financial merits, rather than relying solely on emotion or hearsay. There's a saying from Robert Kawasaki — the famous author of *Rich Dad, Poor Dad*:

"When emotions go up, intelligence goes down."

Kawasaki's quote is important because it is true; using intelligence enables investors to manage their real estate investments effectively. Budgeting for property maintenance and repairs, managing rental income and expenses, and making strategic decisions about when to buy, sell, or hold a property are all key parts of being financially literate as a real estate investor and landlord.

Real estate investors are able to compartmentalize their emotions in order to logically assess the risks and rewards of a real estate investment and make informed decisions about whether to invest, how much to invest, and how to finance the investment. They don't allow things such as "passion" to take control of their minds because then they run the risk of throwing logic (and potentially hundreds of thousands of dollars) out the window.

Understanding and evaluating the potential risks for a property while considering the potential rewards for a property is absolutely essential for minimizing financial risks associated with real estate investing. This includes understanding depreciation and capital gains taxes, and taking steps to protect your investment through property insurance and risk management strategies.

As a potential long distance landlord, here are some ways that you can improve you financial literacy:

- *Read books and articles on real estate investing and personal finance:* There are many books and articles available that can help you to improve your financial literacy. These resources can provide valuable insights on topics such as property valuation, financing options, tax implications, and cash flow analysis.

- *Attend workshops and seminars:* Many real estate investing and personal finance workshops and seminars are available both in-person and online. Attending these events allow you to learn from experts in the field, ask questions, and network with other real estate professionals.

- *Seek guidance from financial advisors or mentors:* Financial advisors or mentors who are experienced in real estate investing can provide valuable insights and advice on financial matters related to being a landlord. These individuals can offer guidance on financial strategies, tax planning, and risk management. It's truly in your best interest to obtain one.

- *Practice active financial management:* Actively managing your finances is one of the best ways to improve financial literacy. This involves keeping detailed records of rental income and expenses, creating a budget, and regularly reviewing financial statements to track cash flow and profitability. If you can't manage your own finances, then it is going to be hard to manage one for the business you're trying to create as a long distance millionaire.

- *Join real estate investing groups:* Joining real estate investing groups, such as local real estate investment clubs helps you to gain more insight on the market, build a network, and get your head in alignment with your millionaire goals.

Scarcity Mindset vs. Abundance Mindset

Imagine a person who goes by Chris. Because they had to take up odd jobs here and there to make ends meet, Chris was excited to finally be able to secure a job that paid twice as much as they previously got paid and quickly disregarded their dream of attending a live, in-person real estate workshop from a prominent figure developer in their city. Chris lives paycheck to paycheck, but often wonders what their life would be like if they invested in that workshop.

As the internet often does, the same day that Chris looked up that real estate mogul, an advertisement popped up showing the next live, in-person real estate workshop coming up in two months. Chris goes back and forth, letting their emotions about their financial insecurity get in the way of their ability to practice risk tolerance. Chris comes up with different reasons why they shouldn't invest in themselves and attend the workshop — some of which being that bills are due soon, they'd have to take off work, they don't have any nice clothes to wear there, so on and so forth. Chris ultimately decides not to attend the event although they know it may change their life.

A scarcity mindset is a belief that there are limited resources or opportunities available, and that one must compete with others to acquire them. People who have a scarcity mindset tend to view the world as a zero-sum game, where success is only possible by taking resources or opportunities away from others. In Chris' case, scarcity mindset looks like focusing on surviving the day-to-day struggles instead of thriving in the long term. You probably know someone who thinks like Chris, don't you?

A scarcity mindset can manifest in several ways. For example, an investor with a scarcity mindset may feel that there are only a limited number of good investment opportunities available and that they must act quickly to secure them. This mindset can lead to impulsive decision-making and a lack of thorough research or due diligence. It can also lead to a lack of collaboration, mistrust, and missed opportunities. Real estate investing requires a long-term perspective and a willingness to work with others to achieve success.

By focusing solely on competition and scarcity, you may miss out on valuable opportunities for collaboration and growth.

To overcome a scarcity mindset, cultivate an abundance mindset instead. An abundance mindset focuses on the idea that there are unlimited resources and opportunities available. This mindset can lead to a more collaborative, supportive approach to real estate investing, where you work with others to achieve success. Focusing on long-term goals and developing a strategic plan can help you avoid the impulse to act quickly and make uninformed decisions.

An abundance mindset is a way of thinking that focuses on the belief that there are plenty of opportunities and resources available for everyone, and that success and happiness are not limited resources. It requires knowing that you can create opportunities and achieve your goals through hard work, persistence, and a positive attitude.

This means that you have to open yourself up to new experiences and, even if you are afraid, become determined to take more risks than you have before or try new approaches to old experiences. Most importantly, it helps you to be less discouraged by setbacks or failures and more determined to accomplish your goal of becoming a long distance landlord and millionaire. Cultivating an abundance mindset lets you focus on opportunities rather than limitations, and to create a positive and optimistic outlook on life. This can lead to greater success, happiness, and fulfillment in all aspects of life, not just your career in real estate investing.

That being said, developing an abundance mindset is a process that requires intentional effort and consistent practice. Here are some tips that you can use to develop an abundance mindset:

- *Practice gratitude:* Cultivating gratitude is a key element of developing an abundance mindset. Focusing on what you already have and what you have achieved so that you can build a sense of abundance and positivity. You can start by making a daily habit of reflecting on what you are grateful for and writing it down.

- *Focus on solutions:* Instead of dwelling on problems or obstacles, landlords with an abundance mindset focus on finding solutions. Approach challenges with a growth mindset, seeing them as opportunities to learn and improve. You can train yourself to shift your focus to solutions by reframing negative thoughts and asking yourself, "What can I do to solve this problem?"

- *Surround yourself with positivity:* Positive people and environments can help you to maintain an abundance mindset. Seek out supportive friends, mentors, or business partners who encourage and inspire you. Create an environment that fosters positivity and abundance by surrounding yourself with inspiring quotes or images, or listening to motivational podcasts or audiobooks.

- *Take calculated risks:* Taking calculated risks is an important part of building an abundance mindset. Challenge yourself to step outside your comfort zone and take on new opportunities, such as purchasing a new rental property or exploring new investment strategies. By taking calculated risks, you can build confidence and develop a "can-do" attitude.

- *Celebrate successes:* Celebrating successes, no matter how small, is an important part of developing an abundance mindset. Take time to acknowledge your achievements and recognize the progress you have made towards your goals. By celebrating successes, you can build momentum and reinforce a positive, abundance-focused mindset.

Lack of focus vs focus

A lack of focus refers to a situation where an individual has difficulty concentrating on a specific task or goal. It can be caused by several things, including a lack of clear goals, competing priorities, external distractions, or mental illnesses such as attention deficit hyperactivity disorder (ADHD) or clinical depression. Many people fail to overcome it because it often requires discipline, time-management skills, and a willingness to prioritize tasks.

Lack of focus can be particularly problematic because real estate investing requires a significant amount of time, energy, and attention to detail. Investors must be able to research potential investments, analyze market trends, and negotiate deals effectively. Without focus, investors may miss critical details, make poor investment decisions, or miss out on valuable opportunities. However, it is essential to address a lack of focus to achieve success in real estate investing. Setting clear goals and priorities, eliminating distractions, and developing effective time-management skills can help you stay focused and make progress towards their goals. Additionally, seeking out mentors or support networks can provide valuable guidance and accountability, helping you stay on track and achieve success in their real estate investing endeavors.

As a landlord, your primary goal is to make a profit from your rental property. Shifting your mindset helps you understand what you need to do to achieve this goal. It involves creating a business plan, setting rental rates that will cover your expenses, and identifying your target market. Without a clear goal, you are likely to make costly mistakes that could harm your financial stability.

Focus is the ability to direct your attention and energy towards a specific task or goal, while minimizing distractions and avoiding multitasking. For potential landlords, focus is a crucial skill that can help them to stay organized, manage their time effectively, prioritize tasks, and achieve their investment goals. Here are some tips that you can use to develop your focus:

- *Set clear goals:* Setting clear and specific goals is essential for maintaining focus. Identify your investment goals, such as acquiring a certain number of properties, achieving a specific rate of return, or increasing their passive income. Once you have set your goals, break them down into smaller, achievable tasks.

- *Create a schedule:* Creating a schedule is a powerful tool for staying focused and organized. Block out specific times in your day or week for tasks such as property searches, meetings with real estate agents or property managers, and financial planning. By creating a schedule, you can prioritize your time and ensure that you are making progress towards your goals.

- *Minimize distractions:* Distractions can disrupt focus and reduce productivity. Identify your distractions, such as social media or email notifications, and take steps to minimize them. This may involve turning off notifications, using apps or tools to block distracting websites, or finding a quiet and distraction-free workspace.

- *Practice mindfulness:* Mindfulness is the practice of being fully present and engaged in the moment. It can help you to stay focused on tasks and avoid getting caught up in distractions or negative thoughts. Techniques such as meditation, deep breathing, or simply taking a few moments to pause and reflect can help to cultivate mindfulness and improve focus.

- *Take breaks:* Taking regular breaks is essential for maintaining focus and avoiding burnout. Schedule regular breaks into your day or week to rest, recharge, and engage in activities that help you to relax and stay focused.

By focusing on developing these mindset characteristics, you can shift your mindset towards becoming a successful landlord in the real estate industry. It is important to recognize that developing these characteristics takes time, effort, and a willingness to learn and grow. However, with perseverance and dedication, anyone can shift their mindset and achieve success in real estate investing. If I did it, you can too. Most importantly, these characteristics will help you to increase your chances of becoming not just a successful landlord, but a good long distance millionaire landlord.

Based on these mindset shifts we went over, you probably creating a mental checklist of a good landlord and a bad one, and to be honest, it's (mostly) objective. A good landlord is someone who provides a safe, comfortable, and well-maintained living space for their tenants, while also respecting their tenants' privacy and rights. They are responsive to tenant concerns and complaints, and take action to address any issues that arise. They also follow all relevant laws and regulations, and maintain open and honest communication with their tenants.

On the other hand, a bad landlord is someone who neglects their properties and fails to provide a safe and comfortable living environment for their tenants. They may be slow to respond to tenant concerns or may ignore them altogether, and may even violate their tenants' privacy or rights. They may also engage in unethical or illegal practices, such as discrimination, harassment, or charging illegal fees.

Good Landlord Characteristics	Bad Landlord Characteristics
Maintain their properties in good condition	Neglect their properties or fail to maintain them in good condition
Respond promptly to tenant requests and concerns	Unnecessarily ignore or delay responding to tenant requests and concerns
Respect their tenants' privacy and rights	Violate their tenants' privacy or rights
Follow all relevant laws and regulations	Engage in discriminatory or harassing behavior
Keep open and honest communication with their tenants	Charge illegal or excessive fees
Treat their tenants with respect and professionalism	Use aggressive or intimidating tactics to collect rent or resolve disputes
Provide fair and reasonable rent prices	Provide poor living conditions or unsafe environments
Conduct regular property inspections and make necessary repairs	Refuse to make necessary repairs or improvements

Ultimately, you can choose your own definition of what a good or bad landlord is, but overall, being a good landlord requires a commitment to maintaining high standards for property management, respecting tenants' rights and privacy, and providing a safe and comfortable living environment. That is undeniable.

If your tenants aren't coming to you with problems often and are paying their rent on time, guess what? You and your team are doing a great job and you most likely have earned the right to call yourself a good landlord.

If the opposite is true after going through this book, then you most likely have not and need to reread this chapter.

Chapter Two: Networking with Realtors and Mortgage Professionals in New Markets

In the exciting world of real estate investing, networking plays a crucial role in finding lucrative deals and establishing valuable connections. In this chapter, we will explore effective strategies for networking with realtors and mortgage professionals in new markets. By building relationships with these professionals, you can gain access to off-market deals, financing opportunities, and valuable market insights.

Networking allows you to get closer to the source of a deal in a new market, which is the seller. While using a realtor is often the easiest way to connect with sellers, there are other strategies worth considering. We'll discuss the benefits of networking and how it can help you navigate new markets successfully.

One strategy to get closer to sellers is through direct marketing campaigns. We'll explore methods such as direct mail campaigns, text campaigns, and driving for dollars using data lists from reputable websites like listsource.com or propstream.com. These campaigns allow you to contact sellers directly and potentially negotiate deals for your landlord portfolio. Here are some ways landlords can utilize these methods and leverage data lists to enhance their marketing:

Direct Marketing Campaigns

Direct Mail

Create targeted direct mail campaigns by sending personalized letters or postcards to property owners in specific neighborhoods or areas of interest. The mailings can highlight your interest in buying properties and provide your contact information for interested sellers to reach out. This can easily be done via USPS by asking them to mail out postcards to a specific zip code. It's not the cheapest, but it can be very effective.

Targeted Online Advertising

Use online advertising platforms, such as social media ads or search engine marketing, to target specific demographics or geographic areas.

Craft compelling ads that highlight your ability to buy properties quickly and hassle-free. Facebook, Google, and Instagram ads are what I'd recommend, but if you're not on social media like that, you should definitely hire someone who is able to produce results when it comes to social media marketing.

Bandit Signs

Place eye-catching bandit signs in high-traffic areas or neighborhoods where you want to invest. These signs typically contain a simple message, such as "We Buy Houses for Cash," along with your contact information. You can print these ad FedEx or Staples. You can also order generic ones from Amazon.

Text Campaigns

SMS Marketing

Build a database of potential sellers' phone numbers and use SMS marketing platforms to send targeted text messages. Craft concise and compelling messages that capture sellers' attention and encourage them to reach out for a potential sale. Some good SMS software include TextMagic and EZ Texting.

Lead Generation Websites

Utilize lead generation websites where sellers can submit their contact information, including their phone numbers, in exchange for an offer or information about selling their property. Follow up with these leads through text messages to initiate conversations and negotiate deals.

Driving for Dollars and Data Lists

Driving for Dollars

Drive through neighborhoods or areas of interest and look for properties in visible distress or signs of potential sellers (e.g., overgrown lawns, boarded-up windows). Take note of these properties and collect their addresses for further research and outreach.

Data Lists

Purchase or access data lists from reliable sources, such as real estate data providers like listsource.com or propstream.com. These data lists can include information about property owners, their contact details, property characteristics, and other relevant data. Use this information to target specific sellers or properties for your marketing campaigns.

When connecting with sellers through these methods, it's crucial to have a compelling value proposition, communicate your expertise and ability to offer fair deals, and provide clear and convenient ways for sellers to contact you. Building rapport and establishing trust with potential sellers will increase the chances of successful lead generation and ultimately closing deals.

There are also other ways to network with sellers. Be sure to bookmark this page because this is important:

REIA Meetings

Attending Real Estate Investment Association (REIA) meetings in the new market can be highly advantageous. REIA meetings provide opportunities to connect with local active investors who have a deep understanding of the market. These investors often have relationships with realtors and wholesalers, making them valuable sources of information and potential deal opportunities.

Real Estate Agent Mixers

Real estate agent mixers offer another avenue for networking in new markets. By attending these events, you can connect with local agents who have expertise in the area and access to a wide range of properties. Building relationships with agents who understand the needs of investors can lead to fruitful collaborations and access to exclusive listings.

Local Banks and Credit Unions

Reaching out to local banks and credit unions can provide insights into active investors, agents, and lenders in the new market. These institutions often have connections to real estate professionals who specialize in investment properties. By establishing relationships with lenders, you can explore financing options tailored to your investment goals.

Leveraging Online Platforms

In addition to in-person networking, online platforms can also be valuable resources for connecting with realtors and mortgage professionals in new markets. Social media platforms, real estate forums, and professional networking websites can help you find and engage with professionals who are active in the target market. Building an online presence and participating in relevant discussions can expand your network and open doors to new opportunities.

Developing Trust and Building Rapport

When networking with realtors and mortgage professionals, it's essential to develop trust and build rapport. This involves demonstrating professionalism, active listening, and showing genuine interest in their expertise. By approaching these professionals with respect and professionalism, you can foster meaningful relationships that benefit both parties.

Providing Value to Your Network

Networking is a two-way street. It's important to offer value to your network of realtors and mortgage professionals as well. Share your knowledge, insights, and experiences with others, and be willing to provide referrals and recommendations when appropriate. Building a reputation as a resourceful and helpful investor will enhance your credibility and strengthen your network.

Nurturing Long-Term Relationships

Networking is not a one-time activity but an ongoing process. It's crucial to nurture the relationships you've built with realtors and mortgage professionals for long-term success. Regular communication, updates on your investment progress, and maintaining a genuine interest in their success will solidify your connections and ensure they continue to support your investing journey.

Expanding Your Network Continuously

To maximize your opportunities in new markets, it's important to continually expand your network. Attend industry conferences, seminars, and local real estate events to meet new professionals and expand your knowledge base. By consistently seeking new connections, you'll increase your chances of discovering unique opportunities and building a robust network.

Networking with realtors and mortgage professionals in new markets is a valuable strategy for real estate investors. By leveraging various avenues, such as direct marketing, attending REIA meetings, engaging with local banks, and utilizing online platforms, you can establish meaningful connections and gain access to exclusive deals and financing options. Approach networking with professionalism, provide value to your network, and nurture relationships for long-term success. With a strong network by your side, you'll be well-equipped to thrive in new markets and achieve your real estate investment and long-distance landlord goals.

Chapter Three: Analyzing Properties

Investing in real estate is a significant financial commitment, and you want to make sure that your investment is profitable. Analyzing a rental property helps you determine the potential rental income, expenses, and cash flow, which are all critical factors in determining profitability. For example, if the property requires extensive repairs or renovations, it could significantly impact your expenses and profitability. However, if you identify areas where the property may require repairs or renovations, you can use that information to negotiate a fair price that reflects the property's true value.

I'll tell you a story about one of my first and worst experiences as a landlord. On December 16, 2017, nearing Christmas, I purchased two properties simultaneously. I figured that since they weren't in poor shape, I'd have all of the boiler and mechanical issues knocked out in the following spring because to my knowledge, it wasn't an urgent matter. What actually happened? Murphy's Law. Everything that could go wrong went wrong way before the spring.

Ten days later, on December 26, I get a phone call from one of the tenants at 5:00 or 6:00am. "The heat is off, and it's cold in here. I need it fixed now!"

It's the day after Christmas, it's the middle of winter, and I'm 2 hours away at home in New York. I now have to find someone who's not with their family during the Christmas holiday to figure out the issue. Hopefully, they can get to a store to find parts and then repair it within a reasonable time frame to get the heat back on. You don't want a person going into multiple nights with no heat in the winter—especially if they have kids in the house.

All of this is happening, and it's ten days after I bought my first rentals. The control freak in me starts going wild at this point. What do I do in this worst-case scenario of no heat in the winter?

It's hard to fix things when it's cold. People charge excessively because they know there aren't many options and they know that it is a pressing issue. Luckily, I had a referral of a family friend who was a handy guy. He went there and looked at it. He says, "Oh, it's just something simple, it's an easy fix. I have to go to the plumbing store, buy it, switch it out, and it should be back on." He got it back on within a couple of hours, plus it only cost me a few hundred dollars instead of the $8,000 I convinced myself that it would cost to fix.

I had to be prepared to have some reserve money set aside just in case, and then two, I had to know who to call if this happened again. That was my make-or-break moment as a long-distance landlord because that experience showed me whether I could be in this business long-term. Going into being a landlord, that was my worst fear. And it happened within ten days that I bought the place. Keep in mind that I hadn't even collected rent at that point, yet.

That same scenario happened to me again in the winter of 2022. I tell people all the time, when you first buy a property, your first twelve months is like having a brand-new baby. Of course, parents will understand that analogy better than someone who doesn't have a kid, but in your first twelve months, you don't know what's about to happen with this kid.

And every single property is like a new kid. You have to go through all the seasons to see what's happening. So I bought a property in March of 2022. You use heat sparingly in the spring. So we fast forward to my first winter with the building, and this thing is running through oil like it's drinking water. I mean, it's constantly going because it has to heat up a big space... and I just don't think the building was set up properly. Which, again, is something I didn't know because this was my first property that had oil in it. Everything I had previously had operated on gas.

I'm about six years in at that point and still dealing with new challenges. However, those challenges were overcome; now I know not to buy anything with oil, or at the very least, to schedule an oil-to-gas conversion with Del Marva the day I buy a property. There's an incredible amount of paperwork involved, but the long-term savings are worth it.

I shared that story to emphasize that buying a property to rent out can be a great investment opportunity for those looking to generate passive income and build long-term wealth. However, the process of analyzing and purchasing a property can be overwhelming, especially for new landlords. Here are a few key steps that you need to take to ensure that you're moving in the right direction.

Define Your Investment Goals

Before you start analyzing properties, it's important to define your investment goals. Are you looking for a property with a high cash flow, or are you more interested in long-term appreciation? Are you looking for a property that you can improve and resell for a profit, or do you want to hold onto the property for the long-term? Defining your investment goals will help you focus your search and make more informed decisions.

Analyze Market Trends

Once you've defined your investment goals, it's important to analyze market trends in the area where you're considering buying a property. Look at historical data on property values, rental rates, and vacancy rates to get a sense of how the market is performing. You can also talk to local real estate agents and property managers to get a sense of the demand for rental properties in the area.

Calculate the Cap Rate

The cap rate is a key metric that can help you determine whether a property is a good investment. The cap rate is calculated by dividing the property's net operating income (NOI) by its purchase price. The NOI is the total income generated by the property, minus all operating expenses, such as property taxes, insurance, and maintenance costs.

Net Operating Income / Purchase Price = Cap Rate

A higher cap rate indicates a higher potential return on investment, but it's important to remember that a high cap rate doesn't necessarily mean a property is a good investment. Other factors, such as the condition of the property, the location, and the demand for rental properties in the area, should also be considered.

Another way to do this is by using the 1% rule. Take 1% of the purchase price. If the rent for the market is higher than that number this property may be a good candidate for investment. (If the property can pass a 2% rule then you should most likely buy that property.)

Formula: Purchase Price x 1% > Market Rent

Example: $250,000 x 1% = $2,500 < $2,000 (Good Investment)

$300,000 x 1% = $3,000 > $2,000 (Poor Investment)

Consider the Location

The location of the property is a key factor to consider when analyzing and buying a property. Look for properties that are located in desirable neighborhoods with good schools, easy access to public transportation, and a low crime rate. Properties that are located near major employers or universities may also be in high demand.

Evaluate the Condition of the Property

Before you buy a property, it's important to evaluate its condition. Look for properties that are well-maintained and in good condition, as these properties are less likely to require major repairs or renovations. It's also important to have the property inspected by a professional to identify any potential issues that may need to be addressed before you purchase the property.

Assess the Rental Potential

When analyzing a property, it's important to assess its rental potential. Look at the rental rates of comparable properties in the area to get a sense of how much you can charge for rent. It's also important to consider the vacancy rate in the area, as a high vacancy rate can make it difficult to find tenants.

Calculate Your Cash Flow

After you've analyzed the property and assessed its rental potential, it's important to calculate your cash flow. Your cash flow is the amount of money you have left over after paying all expenses, including mortgage payments, property taxes, insurance, and maintenance costs. A positive cash flow indicates a profitable investment, while a negative cash flow indicates that the property is costing you money.

Secure Financing

Once you've found a property that meets your investment goals and analyzed its potential, it's time to secure financing. Talk to local banks and mortgage lenders to get pre-approved for a loan. Shop around for the best interest rates and terms. Remember: the more money you put as a down payment, the lower your mortgage payment is, and the higher your cash flow will be. With that being said, there are several types of loan options available for potential landlords, each with its own benefits and requirements. Here are some of the most common types of loans for rental properties:

Conventional mortgages are best for borrowers with good credit and stable income who are looking to purchase a rental property. Since these loans are not backed by the government, they typically require higher credit scores and higher down payments than government-backed loans.

Conventional mortgages may be a good option for borrowers who have a down payment of 15-20% and want to avoid paying mortgage insurance premiums. These loans may also offer lower interest rates than government-backed loans, which can save borrowers money over the life of the loan. However, it's important to note that conventional mortgages may have stricter requirements for the rental property itself. For example, the property may need to meet certain occupancy and income requirements, and the borrower may need to have a certain amount of cash reserves on hand.

Overall, conventional mortgages are a good option for borrowers who have strong credit and finances and are willing to meet the stricter requirements for the loan and the rental property. Keep in mind that there is a cap on the number of properties you will be able to get loans for. This is known as the "number of properties financed" limit and is usually set around ten.

If you're already a landlord with multiple properties, you may need to consider other options.

A hard money loan, also known as a private money loan, is a type of financing used by real estate investors to purchase or renovate a property quickly. Hard money loans are typically secured by the property itself and are often provided by private lenders or investors, rather than traditional banks or mortgage lenders.

Hard money loans are called "hard" because they are typically secured by a hard asset, such as real estate, as opposed to traditional loans that are secured by a borrower's creditworthiness or income. Hard money lenders are often private individuals or companies that lend money based on the value of the property being purchased or renovated, rather than the borrower's financial history or credit score.

The terms of hard money loans can vary depending on the lender and the specific property being financed. However, they typically have shorter repayment periods and higher interest rates than traditional loans. Hard money loans may also require a larger down payment, and the lender may only finance a portion of the property's value.

Hard money loans are often used by real estate investors who need to move quickly on a property or who plan to renovate and flip the property for a quick profit. They can be a good option for investors who have a solid exit strategy and are confident in their ability to generate a return on their investment quickly. However, investors should carefully consider the costs and risks associated with hard money loans before deciding to use this type of financing.

Other types of loans for specific demographics include:

- *FHA loans:* Federal Housing Administration (FHA) loans are government-backed loans designed to help low-to-moderate-income borrowers purchase homes. FHA loans may require a lower down payment than conventional mortgages, but they may also require mortgage insurance premiums and have stricter property requirements.

- *VA loans:* Veterans Affairs (VA) loans are government-backed loans designed to help veterans and their families purchase homes. These loans often require no down payment and may offer competitive interest rates.

- *USDA loans:* United States Department of Agriculture (USDA) loans are government-backed loans designed to help borrowers in rural areas purchase homes. These loans may offer no down payment and low-interest rates.

When considering loan options for a rental property, evaluate the requirements and benefits of each option to find the best fit for your financial situation and investment goals.

Once you have analyzed each potential property based on these factors, you can make an informed decision on which property to buy. Investing in real estate is a long-term commitment, and it's important to choose properties that have the potential to generate consistent rental income and appreciate in value over time.

In addition to analyzing and buying properties, there are other considerations for new landlords. We discuss these in upcoming chapters, but keep this in mind:

Legal requirements

Before taking the plunge into owning and managing a rental property, it's crucial to have a solid grasp of the legal landscape in your state or local jurisdiction. Familiarize yourself with the intricacies of landlord-tenant laws to ensure you understand the rights and responsibilities of both parties involved. Stay abreast of fair housing laws to avoid any unintentional discrimination in your rental practices.

Additionally, delve into the relevant building codes governing rental properties in your area. Understanding these codes not only ensures compliance but also contributes to the safety and habitability of your rental units. Staying well-versed in these legal requirements serves as a foundation for responsible and effective property management, protecting both you and your tenants while fostering a positive and legally sound rental experience.

Tenant screening

Establishing a comprehensive tenant screening process is pivotal in securing trustworthy and responsible tenants for your rental property. Craft a thorough procedure encompassing key elements such as a detailed rental application. This application should delve into tenants' rental history, employment, and personal information. Conduct a credit check to assess their financial stability, ensuring they have a history of meeting financial obligations. A criminal background check is equally essential to guarantee the safety and well-being of your property and other tenants. Don't overlook the significance of collecting references from past landlords or employers, offering valuable insights into an applicant's reliability and conduct. By diligently implementing these screening measures, you not only protect your investment but also cultivate a positive and secure living environment for both your tenants and the community.

Property management

When contemplating the management of your rental property, especially if you envision owning multiple properties or residing at a considerable distance from your investment, it's worth exploring the option of hiring a professional property manager. A seasoned property manager can efficiently handle the day-to-day responsibilities, from overseeing tenant relations and property maintenance to addressing unforeseen issues that may arise. This not only alleviates the burden of hands-on management but also ensures that your properties are well-maintained and tenants are content. Property managers bring expertise in navigating legalities, handling finances, and implementing effective marketing strategies. By enlisting their services, you streamline operations, maximize the value of your investments, and potentially free up time for further property acquisitions or personal pursuits.

Insurance

When acquiring a rental property, it's imperative to secure sufficient insurance coverage to safeguard against potential liability issues and property damage. Invest time in thoroughly researching and selecting a comprehensive insurance policy that aligns with the specific needs of your property. This typically includes coverage for property damage caused by events such as natural disasters or accidents, as well as liability protection in case of injury or damage occurring on the premises. Adequate insurance not only provides financial security but also ensures that you are well-protected from unforeseen circumstances, offering peace of mind throughout your tenure as a property owner.

By considering factors such as location, property condition, rental income, expenses, financing, cash flow, and ROI, you can make informed decisions that lead to profitable investments. Additionally, it's important to understand the legal requirements, develop a thorough tenant screening process, consider hiring a property manager, and purchase adequate insurance coverage to protect yourself and your investment. With the right mindset, skills, and knowledge, you will become a successful landlord and build a profitable real estate portfolio.

Chapter Four: Buying Properties

As an aspiring landlord, one of the key challenges you'll face is finding the right properties to add to your portfolio. In the last chapter, I shared several ways that you can maximize your network to land opportunities. In this chapter, I'll delve into the various avenues you can explore to discover properties that align with your investment goals. From traditional methods to short sales, you have a range of options to help you find the perfect properties to purchase.

Here are some of the different ways that you can buy properties. Remember, your network will be extremely valuable and still should be used in tandem with your own search efforts.

Traditional Purchase

This involves finding a property on the market and making an offer to buy it. This method typically involves working with a real estate agent and financing the purchase with a mortgage.

Pros:
- Expertise: Real estate agents and brokers possess industry knowledge and expertise, guiding you through the purchasing process and providing valuable insights.
- Access to Listings: Working with professionals gives you access to a broader range of property listings, increasing the chances of finding suitable investment opportunities.
- Negotiation Skills: Experienced agents can negotiate on your behalf, potentially securing favorable purchase terms, price reductions, or additional concessions.
- Established Processes: Traditional property purchases follow well-defined procedures, ensuring a structured and regulated transaction process.
- Market Insight: Agents can provide market analysis and data to help you make informed decisions about property values, rental rates, and investment potential.

Cons:

- Commission Fees: Real estate agents typically charge commissions, which can range from 2% to 6% of the property's sale price. This expense reduces your overall return on investment.
- Limited Control: Relying on an agent means relinquishing some control over the purchasing process. You may have less direct involvement in property selection, negotiation, and decision-making.
- Competitive Environment: The traditional market can be highly competitive, especially for desirable properties in sought-after locations. Multiple offers may drive up prices and limit your bargaining power.
- Reliance on Others: Depending on professionals means relying on their availability and commitment. Delays or miscommunication from agents or brokers can slow down the purchasing process.
- Higher Costs: Traditional property purchases often involve higher upfront costs, including down payments, closing costs, and potential expenses for property inspections and appraisals.

Auction

Buying a property at an auction can be a good way to get a deal, but it requires careful preparation and research. Properties at auction are often sold as-is, with no opportunity for inspections or contingencies.

Pros:

- Potential Bargains: Auctions can provide opportunities to purchase properties at lower prices compared to traditional market transactions. Distressed properties or foreclosures may be available, offering potential discounts.
- Efficient Process: Auctions often have a streamlined and time-limited process, allowing for a quicker purchase compared to traditional methods. Once the auction concludes, successful bidders can proceed with the transaction promptly.
- Transparency: Auctions typically offer a transparent bidding process, where participants can see competing bids and adjust their offers accordingly. This transparency can provide a fair and open platform for acquiring properties.

- Variety of Properties: Auctions may feature a wide range of properties, including residential, commercial, or undeveloped land. This variety gives buyers more options to find properties that align with their investment goals.
- Potential for Profit: If you can secure a property at a favorable price, there may be potential for profit through resale, rental income, or property appreciation.

Cons:
- Limited Inspection Time: Auction properties often have limited or no access for property inspections before the auction. This lack of thorough examination can increase the risk of unforeseen issues or repair costs after the purchase.
- Competitive Environment: Auctions can be highly competitive, with multiple bidders vying for the same property. This competition can drive up prices and diminish potential savings initially anticipated.
- Cash Requirement: Auction purchases typically require immediate payment or a substantial deposit upon winning the bid. This cash requirement may limit access to financing options and require having sufficient funds readily available.
- Non-Refundable Deposits: Deposits made at auctions are often non-refundable, meaning if you win the bid but later choose not to proceed, you may lose the deposit.
- Limited Due Diligence: The accelerated nature of auctions may limit the time available for thorough research and due diligence. Buyers must be prepared to make informed decisions based on the information provided before the auction.

Short sale

In a short sale, the seller owes more on the property than it is worth, and the lender agrees to accept a lower amount to avoid foreclosing. This can be a good opportunity to get a property at a discount, but fair warning, the process can be a little more complicated and lengthy than traditional purchasing.

Pros:

- Potential for Bargain Prices: Short sales occur when the homeowner is unable to meet mortgage obligations, and the lender agrees to sell the property for less than the outstanding loan balance. This can present an opportunity to purchase the property at a discounted price compared to market value.
- Room for Negotiation: Short sales involve negotiations between the seller, lender, and potential buyer. There may be flexibility in negotiating the purchase price, terms, and conditions of the sale, allowing for potential savings or favorable terms.
- Potential for Property Value Appreciation: If the property market experiences appreciation over time, purchasing a property through a short sale may offer the potential for future value growth and equity gains.
- Opportunity for Upgrading or Flipping: Buying a property through a short sale can provide an opportunity to make improvements, renovate, or flip the property for profit.

Cons:

- Lengthy and Uncertain Process: Short sales can involve a lengthy and unpredictable process due to the involvement of multiple parties, including the homeowner, lender, and sometimes even additional lien holders. Delays can occur during negotiations, property inspections, and approval from the lender.
- Limited Control: As a buyer, you have limited control over the short sale process. The decision to accept an offer rests with the lender, and they may reject or counter your offer, leading to potential frustration and disappointment.
- Potential Property Condition Issues: Short sale properties are typically sold "as-is," meaning the seller may not be willing or able to make repairs or disclose all property defects. Conducting thorough inspections and assessments before purchasing becomes crucial to avoid unpleasant surprises.
- Financing Challenges: Financing a short sale purchase can be more complex than a traditional sale. Some lenders may require specific terms or conditions for financing approval, and the buyer must meet those requirements.

- Competing Offers and Bidding Wars: Short sales can attract multiple buyers interested in securing a discounted property. This competition can lead to bidding wars and potentially drive up the purchase price.

Foreclosure

Buying a foreclosed property can also be a good way to get a deal, but it requires careful research and preparation. Foreclosed properties are often sold as-is, and there may be liens or other issues to address.

Pros:
- Potential for Bargain Prices: Foreclosed properties are often sold at a discounted price compared to their market value. This presents an opportunity for buyers to acquire properties at a lower cost, potentially leading to financial savings or investment opportunities.
- Wide Selection of Properties: Foreclosed properties come in various types, including single-family homes, condominiums, multi-unit buildings, and commercial properties. This wide range of options allows buyers to choose properties that align with their investment goals or personal preferences.
- Room for Negotiation: Buyers may have room for negotiation when purchasing foreclosed properties. Banks or lending institutions that own the properties are often motivated to sell and may be open to considering offers below the listed price or negotiating favorable terms.
- Potential for Property Value Appreciation: If the property market experiences appreciation over time, purchasing a foreclosed property may offer the potential for future value growth and equity gains.
- Opportunity for Flipping or Rental Income: Foreclosed properties can be attractive options for real estate investors looking to renovate and resell (flip) or generate rental income. With proper due diligence and strategic planning, these properties can provide profitable ventures.

Cons:

- Property Condition Risks: Foreclosed properties are typically sold "as-is," meaning the buyer may inherit any existing issues or damage. Conducting thorough inspections and assessments becomes crucial to identify potential problems and estimate repair costs accurately.
- Limited Information and Disclosures: Foreclosed properties may lack detailed information about their history, maintenance, or any hidden problems. Buyers need to rely on their own due diligence and inspections to uncover potential issues.
- Lengthy and Complex Buying Process: Purchasing a foreclosed property involves a more intricate process compared to a traditional sale. The involvement of banks or lending institutions, legal procedures, and potential liens can contribute to delays and complexities.
- Financing Challenges: Financing a foreclosed property can be more challenging than a traditional sale. Buyers may face stricter loan requirements, difficulty obtaining financing for properties in poor condition, or limited financing options.
- Title and Legal Issues: Some foreclosed properties may have title or legal complications that could impact the buyer's ownership rights or pose future legal challenges. Conducting a thorough title search and working with experienced professionals can help mitigate these risks.

Off-Market Properties

Some properties are sold without ever being listed on the open market. This can be an opportunity to get a property before it becomes available to the general public, but it requires networking and building relationships with sellers and agents.

Pros:

- Less Competition: Off-market properties are not publicly listed, which means there is typically less competition from other buyers. This can give you an advantage in negotiating favorable terms and potentially securing a property at a lower price.

- Increased Privacy: Off-market transactions offer a higher level of privacy and discretion. Sellers may prefer to keep the sale confidential or avoid the hassle of open houses and public marketing.
- Potential for Unique Deals: Off-market properties may present unique opportunities that are not available on the open market. Sellers may be more flexible in terms of financing options, negotiation terms, or unconventional deals.
- Personalized Approach: Off-market transactions often involve direct communication between the buyer and seller or their representatives. This allows for more personalized negotiations and the ability to tailor the transaction to specific needs and preferences.
- Access to Undiscovered Properties: Off-market purchases provide access to properties that are not widely known or visible to the general public. This can include distressed properties, motivated sellers, or exclusive listings.

Cons:
- Limited Property Pool: Since off-market properties are not publicly listed, the pool of available options may be more limited compared to properties on the open market. This can make finding suitable properties more challenging.
- Difficulty in Finding Opportunities: Identifying off-market properties requires more effort and resources. It may involve networking, building relationships with industry professionals, or using specialized platforms or services to discover hidden opportunities.
- Lack of Price Transparency: Without the public listing and market exposure, off-market properties may not have clear price indicators. It can be harder to assess whether the asking price is fair or competitive, making negotiations more complex.
- Increased Due Diligence: Off-market properties may have limited information available, requiring buyers to conduct more extensive due diligence. This includes obtaining property records, verifying ownership, assessing property condition, and estimating repair costs.

- Potential for Higher Prices: While off-market properties can offer potential deals, they can also be subject to higher prices. Sellers may expect a premium for the privacy and convenience of an off-market transaction.

When pursuing a property purchase, again, it's important to have a proactive approach, build relationships with industry professionals, and leverage various channels to discover potential opportunities. Conducting thorough due diligence, seeking professional advice, and carefully evaluating the property's value and potential risks are critical steps to ensure a successful purchase. Ultimately, the best way to buy a property will depend on your individual circumstances and goals. Do your research and work with professionals who can help guide you through the process. I talk more about this in chapter thirteen.

Chapter Five: Making Offers

After analyzing a property, the next step is to make an offer on the property. This is the process of communicating your intention to purchase the property to the seller.

Depending on how you have been communicating with the sellers will determine which way the offer is being made and who is actually doing it. If you are using a realtor as a buyers' agent or the seller's agent, the realtor will be the one drafting and submitting your written offer to the seller. When the seller receives your LOI (letter of intent), they may accept your offer, reject it, or make a counteroffer.

Negotiations may take place until both parties come to an agreement. During this process, you may need to make concessions or adjustments to your offer to come to a mutually acceptable agreement. I would like to be clear about something for all of my new aspiring investors and maybe some of my veterans—there are a million different things that can be put into a real estate contract as a contingency requirement, so as my uncle used to say to me when I was a young, mischievous child:

"You never know until you ask…"

That saying applies to real estate when making offers and negotiating things to be in included or excluded in a contract. Some standard things that are included in a contingency in a contract will be mortgage contingency, inspection contingency and appraisal contingency to name a few. Each of those items will provide you with the opportunity to cancel a contract if there are any issues with the contingency item.

For example under the mortgage contingency. Let's say you are purchasing an investment property with a loan which is perfectly normal, but for whatever reason you do not get approved for the mortgage you applied for to purchase the property. If this denial of the mortgage happens within the specified time frame that is outlined in the contract you can then cancel the deal because it did not get approved for your mortgage and you will receive your earnest money deposit (EMD) back from the deal. Essentially, the contingency gives you multiple ways out of a deal to not lose your deposit.

Once an offer has been accepted, the due diligence period begins. This is the time when you, as the buyer, conduct a thorough investigation of the property. This includes a home inspection, a title search, and any necessary financial analysis. The results of this investigation may affect the final offer price or the decision to move forward with the purchase.

Once due diligence is complete, and all contingencies have been met, the final step is to close the deal. This involves signing the necessary documents and paying the purchase price. The closing process is typically handled by a real estate attorney or a licensed real estate agent.

By understanding the market, determining a fair offer price, and negotiating the terms of the sale, you can make a successful offer on a rental property. It is important to work with experienced professionals, such as real estate agents and attorneys, throughout the process to ensure a smooth and successful transaction.

Let me share a story with you.

I had a client who was buying a house. I was the agent representing them on a purchase, and the seller's attorney was the worst attorney I have ever seen in my life.

The attorney almost killed the transaction. It was that bad. The client was a tenant interested in purchasing a house from their landlord. As an agent, you have to be really careful what you say to people, because you're licensed, but things were going so awry that at one point, I had the buyer ask the seller where he got this attorney from because he was not doing his job well. The seller swore up and down that the attorney was doing everything he was supposed to do and that everything was right.

In fact, the landlord/seller told my client, "It's your people. Your people are the ones that are messing things up."

In true Murphy's Law fashion, things got worse under pressure. After the many daisy chains of conversations, we weren't getting anywhere with the deal and I coordinated a Zoom call. I got everybody on the Zoom call; me, the other agent, the buyer, the seller, and both of the attorneys. Five minutes into the call, everyone started to realize just how disorganized the seller's attorney was. He didn't know where the paperwork was, he didn't know what he did for his client, and he had no idea what was going on.

The seller is on the call and is having to clarify and explain who did what and where documents were. It was a complicated sale to begin with, and the attorney just made it worse. After that call, the seller apologized to the tenant and said, "I didn't realize how badly he dropped the ball." We had tried to tell him for three months, and at this point, if he didn't close in the next four weeks, the house was not getting sold and they wouldn't get any more time from the bank.

Then, the attorney quit on him one week before the closing.

The attorney felt that he was being disrespected and everybody allegedly was making him look like the bad guy. So he quit, and told the title company that they weren't closing the transaction anymore.

If you are a new investor I recommend using an attorney or title company depending on the state you are purchasing in. Locating an attorney is best done by using referrals. I tend to ask the seller to give me their current attorney and title company to process the transaction. One of the major benefits of this strategy is that they are already familiar with the property and have records of the property history. You will normally have to sign a waiver allowing the attorney to represent both of you in the transaction but it's mostly about recording the proper documents and transferring ownership. I'm going to use a lot of industry terms in this section, but there's a glossary at the end of the book that defines these words for you. Please stay with me.

Yes, making an offer can be a nerve-wracking experience, especially for first-time real estate investors; but, it doesn't have to be if you have a good team of professionals to work with.

You have an understanding of the market, so you can determine the "offer price" for the property. This is the price you are willing to pay for the property. You can base this price on the property's condition, location, features, and market value. It is important to come up with a realistic offer price that takes into consideration your budget and your long-term investment goals. I suggest that you NEVER start with your max offer when making an offer to a seller or realtor. You always want to give yourself some room to move up so you look as if you are "playing ball" with the other side.

Once you have determined your offer price, the next step is to submit a letter of intent (LOI) to the seller. An LOI is a non-binding agreement that outlines the terms of the offer. It should include the offer price, any contingencies, and the proposed closing date. This document is typically prepared by a licensed real estate agent or real estate attorney.

A realtor or "buyer's agent" in this case, can play an important role in buying property, especially for those who are new to the process. Realtors are licensed professionals who are knowledgeable about the local real estate market and can provide guidance and assistance throughout the buying process by providing guidance on the fair market value of a property and helping negotiate an appropriate price, facilitating property inspections (including inspections for structural issues, pest problems, and other potential concerns), ensure that all necessary documentation is completed accurately and on time, and is legally bound to represent your interests in the transaction and can help protect your rights as a buyer. They can provide advice on the terms of the sale, negotiate on your behalf, and ensure that the closing process goes smoothly. The realtor questionnaire will help you choose the best possible options for your transaction.

A real estate attorney's role in buying property is to provide legal advice and guidance to their clients throughout the transaction. This can include reviewing and negotiating the purchase agreement to ensure that it is fair and reasonable (and that all legal requirements have been met), advising their clients on any issues or potential legal problems that may arise, conducting title searches to ensure that the title is clear and free from any liens or encumbrances that could affect their client's ownership of the property, advising on the legal implications of any contingencies or disclosures that may be included in the purchase agreement, such as inspections, financing, or other requirements, and overseeing the closing process to ensure that all necessary legal documents are properly executed, and that all funds are properly transferred and disbursed.

Hopefully you have gained enough confidence from the previous chapters to start making those offers and getting into those conversations.

Chapter Six: Contractors for Maintenance and Repairs

If you want to navigate the potential pitfalls of your investing business, this chapter is a crucial read. As a real estate investor, one area where many headaches arise is in dealing with contractors and maintenance issues. Countless horror stories circulate about the risks and stress associated with being a landlord. However, by approaching contractor relationships strategically, you can minimize the challenges and make the process as painless as possible. In this chapter, we will explore when to schedule repairs and maintenance, how to properly vet contractors, and where to find them.

Effective Timing for Repairs and Maintenance

Knowing when to schedule repairs and maintenance is crucial for maintaining your properties efficiently. Here are some guidelines to consider:

Preventative Maintenance

Taking a proactive stance on property maintenance involves regular inspections and swift resolution of minor issues. This practice is key to preventing small problems from snowballing into more extensive and expensive repairs. You might recall my story from chapter four. If anyone understands the significance of preventative maintenance, it's yours truly. Embracing this approach is like having an insurance policy for your property's well-being.

By staying on top of inspections and promptly addressing concerns, you not only avoid bigger headaches down the line but also contribute to the long-term health and resilience of your investment. It's a lesson I learned firsthand, and it's a valuable principle to keep in mind for you, too.

Prioritize Urgent Repairs

Handling urgent repairs promptly is crucial to prevent further damage to your property and guarantee the safety and comfort of your tenants. Immediate attention is particularly vital for issues like water leaks, electrical malfunctions, or security concerns.

Trust me, when it comes to urgent repairs, there's no room for delay. Timely action not only safeguards your property from exacerbating issues but also maintains a secure and comfortable environment for your tenants. It also keeps you out of legal trouble.

Strategic Planning

Strategic planning of repairs and maintenance is essential to minimize disruptions for your tenants. Take into account factors such as the lease renewal cycle, seasonal considerations, and tenant preferences when scheduling significant renovations or repairs that may necessitate temporary relocation. Balancing these aspects ensures that major undertakings align with the most convenient times for your tenants, reducing inconveniences and optimizing their living experience.

This thoughtful approach not only showcases your commitment to tenant satisfaction but also contributes to smoother property management, fostering positive landlord-tenant relationships in the long run.

Finding Contractors

One of the most effective ways to find reliable contractors is through word-of-mouth referrals. While it may initially seem challenging if you are new to a market or lack contacts, it is essential to build relationships within the local real estate community. Here are some strategies for finding contractors:

Network within the Local Real Estate Community

Engage with real estate agents, attorneys, and other investors in the market you are looking to invest in. Seek recommendations and referrals from these professionals who have likely worked with contractors in the area.

Tap into the Seller's Network

When purchasing a property, ask the seller about their experiences with contractors. Sellers often have valuable insights into past repairs and maintenance issues, indirectly providing recommendations based on their own experiences.

Seek Referrals from Established Contractors

Once you have established relationships with one or two reliable contractors, ask them for referrals to other contractors with different specialties. Their industry connections can lead you to trustworthy professionals in areas such as carpentry, plumbing, electrical work, HVAC systems, or roofing. These are the most common contractors needed for home repair.

The Contractor Vetting Process

When it comes to hiring contractors, thorough vetting is essential. By asking the right questions and conducting due diligence, you can increase the likelihood of finding reliable and competent professionals. Here are some key considerations during the contractor vetting process:

Experience and Track Record - How long have you been in the business? Where were you trained? What is your specialty? Do you have an in-house team or do you use subcontractors?

Inquire about the contractor's experience in the industry and their track record of completing similar projects successfully. If any one contractor tells you that they do everything, RUN; there's so much that goes into each of the specialized contract work that you'll need that it's impossible for one person to master all of them. Determine if the contractor employs subcontractors or has an in-house team to complete the work. Inquire about the subcontractors' qualifications and their relationship with the contractor.

Licenses and Insurance - Are you licensed and insured? How do you handle permits and regulatory compliance?

Verify that the contractor holds the necessary licenses and permits required for the type of work they will be performing. Ensure they carry liability insurance and worker's compensation coverage to protect yourself from potential liabilities. Ask about the contractor's knowledge and experience in obtaining necessary permits and ensuring compliance with building codes and regulations. Make sure that they are familiar with local requirements and will handle all of the necessary paperwork.

Portfolio and Past Projects - Can you provide references from past clients?

Request a portfolio of their past projects or examples of their work. This will give you an idea of their expertise, craftsmanship, and attention to detail. Reviewing their portfolio can help you assess whether their style aligns with your expectations. Ask for references and follow up with previous clients to gain insights into their work quality and professionalism.

Timelines and Communication - How do you handle project changes or unforeseen issues? What is your preferred method of communication?

Discuss the contractor's availability and their ability to meet project deadlines. Clear communication is crucial, so ask about their preferred methods of communication and how they handle project updates and progress reports.

Contracts and Pricing - Can you provide a detailed estimate and timeline for the project? Can you provide a written contract?

Obtain detailed written contracts outlining the scope of work, project timelines, payment terms, and any warranties or guarantees. Transparent pricing, including a breakdown of costs, will help you evaluate the contractor's estimates and make informed decisions.

By asking these questions, you can gain valuable insights into a contractor's qualifications, experience, professionalism, and ability to meet your project requirements. Remember to trust your instincts and choose a contractor who aligns with your needs and communicates effectively. I always recommend keeping two of each specialty in your back pocket so that you can have multiple quotes and just in case one contractor is busy.

Hiring contractors is a critical aspect of real estate investing, and by approaching it strategically, you can minimize potential challenges. Thoroughly vetting contractors, leveraging word-of-mouth referrals, and understanding the timing for repairs and maintenance will help you build successful partnerships and maintain your properties effectively. While issues may arise, a well-prepared investor can navigate these challenges with confidence, ensuring smoother operations and greater success in the real estate industry.

Chapter Seven: Qualifying Reliable and Responsible Tenants

Selecting the right tenants for your rental property is crucial for a successful landlord-tenant relationship. Making informed decisions during the tenant selection process can help you avoid potential issues and ensure consistent rent payments. In this chapter, we will explore strategies and considerations to help you weed out undesirable applicants and find reliable tenants for your property.

Establishing a Consistent Application Process

Creating a consistent and standardized application process is essential for efficient tenant intake. Whether you're a long-distance or local landlord, the primary goal is to collect monthly rent consistently and without hassle. We'll discuss the benefits of using Section 8 guidelines as a framework for analyzing cash flows and rents, as well as the importance of maintaining a uniform system when qualifying tenants to avoid accusations of discrimination.

Effective Advertising

Effective advertising plays a vital role in attracting prospective tenants to your rental property. Utilizing multiple platforms and websites can significantly increase visibility. Consider posting your listings on platforms like AffordableHousing.com (formerly GoSection8.com) to reach a wide audience. Affordable housing syndicates to multiple websites such as Zillow.com, Trulia.com and several other well known trusted websites that will give your listing plenty of exposure to various types of potential Tenants not only subsidized Section 8 ones. Despite any preconceived notions about Section 8 tenants, it's crucial to evaluate all applicants thoroughly to minimize risk and maximize rental income.

Property Viewing as a Requirement

Requiring prospective tenants to view the property before applying helps filter out non-serious applicants and ensures they are comfortable with the property's location and community. By making property viewing a prerequisite, you can focus on applicants who are genuinely interested in your property, reducing the chances of issues down the line. After the viewing, provide applicants with an application form to be completed on-site, along with an application fee. My go-to application fee is $50. (That is the fee being charged at the time this book was written. Things inevitably will change and become more expensive so adjust your fee according to what is customary for your market.)

Screening for Financial Stability

Determining a tenant's ability to pay rent is a crucial aspect of the tenant selection process. For applicants who do not receive subsidies or program assistance, it's important to establish an income-to-rent ratio qualification. Many landlords and management companies use a rule of thumb, such as requiring the applicant's income to be at least 30 or 40 times the rent amount. However, for Section 8 applicants, it's essential to understand and comply with laws related to protected classes. (I talk more about Section 8 in chapter eleven.)

Conducting Comprehensive Background Checks

To gain insights into applicants' suitability, conducting comprehensive background checks is essential. One recommended online service is MySmartMove.com, owned by TransUnion, which offers various reports to assess applicant qualifications. It's advisable to request and review three reports for each applicant: a credit report, a criminal background report, and a national eviction-related report. These reports provide valuable information about the applicant's financial responsibility, criminal history, and past rental behaviors. You want to avoid renting to applicants that have a history of issues with making payments which would be reflected by having a poor credit score or having a history of being in Landlord Tenant court.

Credit Report

A credit report provides valuable insights into an applicant's financial responsibility and their ability to manage their debts and obligations. Landlords can assess an applicant's payment history, identify any delinquencies or defaults, and make an informed decision about their likelihood of paying rent on time. By reviewing an applicant's credit report, landlords can assess the level of risk associated with renting to that individual. A history of missed payments, high debt levels, or significant financial issues may indicate a higher risk of potential rental payment problems.

While rental payments generally do not appear on credit reports, landlords can still gain insights into an applicant's overall payment patterns. If the applicant has a consistent history of late payments or defaults on other financial obligations, it may raise concerns about their ability to meet their rental obligations. Finally, utilizing credit reports as part of the tenant screening process helps landlords demonstrate a consistent and objective approach to applicant evaluation. This can help ensure compliance with fair housing laws by basing decisions on objective financial criteria rather than personal biases or discriminatory practices. Here are some key components typically included in a credit report:

Personal Information

This section includes the applicant's name, address, Social Security number, date of birth, and employment history. It helps verify the applicant's identity and provides essential background information.

Credit Accounts

The credit report lists the applicant's open and closed credit accounts, such as credit cards, loans, mortgages, and lines of credit. It provides details about the account balance, credit limit, payment history, and any delinquencies or defaults.

Payment History

This section shows the applicant's payment behavior on their credit accounts. It includes information about on-time payments, late payments, missed payments, and any accounts that have gone into collections. Landlords can assess an applicant's reliability in meeting financial obligations by reviewing their payment history.

Credit Inquiries

The credit report lists inquiries made by lenders or creditors when the applicant has applied for credit. Landlords can see if the applicant has recently been seeking credit or loans, which can provide insights into their financial situation and stability.

Public Records

This section includes information from public records, such as bankruptcies, tax liens, judgments, and civil lawsuits. Landlords can assess an applicant's overall financial health and potential risks by reviewing these records.

Credit Score

The credit report often includes a credit score, which is a numerical representation of an applicant's creditworthiness. Credit scores range from poor to excellent and are based on various factors, including payment history, credit utilization, length of credit history, types of credit, and recent credit inquiries. A credit score provides a summary of the applicant's overall creditworthiness and can help landlords evaluate their risk level.

Criminal Background Report

Checking an applicant's criminal background helps ensure the safety and well-being of your property and other tenants. Use this report to identify any previous arrests or convictions and consider these factors when making a decision. By assessing an applicant's criminal history, landlords can identify individuals with a record of violent offenses or other crimes that may pose a risk to the community.

Utilizing criminal background reports as part of the tenant screening process helps landlords demonstrate due diligence and compliance with legal obligations. It ensures that decisions are based on objective factors related to tenant safety and property protection, rather than discriminatory practices. Remember that some insurance providers may require landlords to conduct tenant background checks, including criminal history, as a condition for coverage. Reviewing criminal background reports helps landlords meet these insurance requirements and maintain appropriate coverage for their rental properties. Here are some key components typically included in a criminal background report:

Arrest Records

The report may include information about any arrests made against the individual, indicating the nature of the offense and the date of the arrest. It helps landlords identify if an applicant has a history of criminal involvement.

Convictions

This section provides details about any convictions the applicant may have, including the type of offense, date of conviction, and sentencing information. It helps landlords understand the seriousness and nature of the crimes committed by the applicant.

Pending Charges

If the applicant has any ongoing criminal cases or pending charges, it will be listed in this section. Landlords can consider these factors when assessing an applicant's reliability and potential risks.

Sex Offender Registry

The report may include information from the sex offender registry, identifying if the applicant is a registered sex offender. This information is crucial for landlords to ensure the safety and well-being of other tenants.

Warrants

If there are any outstanding warrants against the applicant, the report may provide details about the warrant, including the issuing agency and the nature of the offense. This information helps landlords identify potential risks associated with renting to the applicant.

National Eviction Report

The national eviction report provides insights into an applicant's past rental history and whether they have been involved in landlord-tenant court cases. This information helps assess the potential risks associated with renting to the applicant. Here are some key components typically included in a national eviction report:

Eviction Filings

The report will list any previous eviction filings against the applicant, indicating the property address, the date of the filing, and the status of the eviction case. This information helps landlords understand if the applicant has a history of being involved in eviction proceedings.

Judgments and Dispositions

If an eviction case resulted in a judgment or disposition, it will be noted in the report. This includes information on whether the tenant was found liable for the eviction, the amount of any monetary judgment, and the terms of the settlement or resolution.

Unlawful Detainers

An unlawful detainer is a legal action taken by a landlord to remove a tenant who refuses to vacate the rental property. The report may include details about any unlawful detainer actions taken against the applicant, providing insights into their past disputes with landlords.

Possession Orders

If a landlord obtained a possession order as part of an eviction process, it will be documented in the report. This indicates that the court granted the landlord the right to take possession of the property after the eviction.

Filing Dates and Dismissals

The report may include information about the dates of eviction filings and whether any of the cases were dismissed or resolved in favor of the tenant. This helps landlords determine the applicant's overall eviction history and the outcomes of previous cases.

Making an Informed Decision

After thoroughly processing and evaluating the applications and background check reports, you can compare applicants based on their income, creditworthiness, and rental history. Consider their overall suitability for the property and make an informed decision on which applicant meets your requirements and qualifies for approval.

Tenant selection is a critical aspect of being a successful landlord. By establishing a consistent application process, utilizing effective advertising strategies, conducting comprehensive background checks, and evaluating applicants based on income and creditworthiness, you can increase your chances of finding reliable and responsible tenants. Remember to comply with fair housing laws and regulations throughout the selection process. By implementing these strategies, you can minimize potential risks and ensure a positive and profitable rental experience.

Chapter Eight: Property Management Procedures

Being a property manager is a crucial yet often undervalued role in the real estate industry. As a buy-and-hold investor, the success of your business and investments heavily relies on the expertise of a skilled property manager. A good manager can maximize occupancy rates, minimize collections issues, and help prevent unnecessary maintenance problems. It's important to recognize that effective property management is paramount to safeguarding your investment and financial well-being. In this chapter, we will explore the key aspects of property management procedures and how they can contribute to your success as a real estate investor and landlord.

The Role of a Property Manager

Being a property manager isn't just about owning buildings – it's about being hands-on and making sure everything runs smoothly. Knowing what a property manager does is key.

One big part of being a property manager is being the go-to person for tenants. When something goes wrong – whether it's a leaky faucet or a power outage – guess who they're going to call? Yep, you! So, being ready to tackle those maintenance issues and handle emergencies is part of the job. How involved you want to be in all this depends on what kind of investor you are and what you're comfortable with. We talk more about this in chapter twelve.

Treating Real Estate as a Business

When it comes to making real money in real estate, you have to treat it like a serious business, not just a side hustle or a hobby. If you want long-term success, you need to establish order and stick to a routine. This isn't just about throwing darts and hoping for the best; it's about creating a solid foundation for managing all those properties you've got your eye on.

Now, imagine this book (and The Long Distance Landlord Workbook) as your trusty toolkit, filled with templates that are like your cheat codes for real estate success. These templates aren't just fancy paperwork

– they're your key to getting things done the right way. Things like collecting rent, dealing with late fees, handling repairs, picking the right tenants, knowing when it's time for eviction, hiring the right folks for the job, and closing out those never-ending maintenance requests – it's all right in these two resources. Following these templates isn't just about being organized; it's about finding your peace of mind in the chaos and bringing some stability to your real estate game.

By sticking to these tried-and-true procedures, you're not just making your life easier; you're building a solid foundation for your real estate empire.

Property Management Procedures

Property managers have a range of tasks that need to be addressed on a monthly, quarterly, and annual basis. These tasks ensure the smooth operation of rental properties and help maintain the financial health of your investments. After all, you don't want to end up having to pay twice for making a mistake once. Here are some common tasks that property managers typically handle on different time frames:

Monthly Tasks

- Rent Collection: Collecting rent from tenants and ensuring timely payment.

- Tenant Communication: Addressing tenant inquiries, concerns, and maintenance requests.

- Property Inspections: Conducting regular inspections to assess the condition of the property and identify any maintenance or repair needs.

- Accounting and Bookkeeping: Maintaining financial records, tracking income and expenses, and preparing monthly financial statements.

- Lease Renewals and Tenant Turnover: Managing lease renewals, coordinating move-ins and move-outs, and addressing vacancies.

- Maintenance and Repairs: Scheduling and overseeing necessary repairs and maintenance work, both routine and emergency.

- Vendor Payments: Processing payments to vendors, contractors, and service providers.

Quarterly Tasks

- Property Inspections: Performing more comprehensive inspections to assess the overall property condition, including common areas and exterior components.

- Lease Reviews: Reviewing existing lease agreements and updating them if necessary.

- Financial Analysis: Analyzing income and expenses, identifying trends, and assessing the property's financial performance.

- Budgeting: Preparing budgets for the upcoming quarter or year, considering anticipated expenses and potential capital improvements.

Annual Tasks

- Lease Renewals and Rent Reviews: Evaluating lease terms and rent rates, negotiating lease renewals, and adjusting rent prices as appropriate.

- Property Tax Assessment: Reviewing property tax assessments and initiating appeals if necessary.

- Insurance Review: Evaluating insurance coverage, comparing policies, and renewing or adjusting coverage as needed.

- Financial Statements and Reporting: Preparing annual financial statements and reports for tax purposes or investor updates.

- Property Maintenance Planning: Assessing long-term maintenance needs, planning and budgeting for major repairs or capital improvements.

- Market Analysis: Conducting a market analysis to evaluate rental rates and property values in the area, ensuring optimal pricing strategies.

- Legal Compliance: Reviewing local laws and regulations, ensuring the property is in compliance, and making any necessary adjustments.

It's important to note that the specific tasks may vary depending on the property type, location, and the scope of services provided by the property manager. Additionally, property managers may handle additional tasks based on individual property owner requirements and the level of service agreement.

Managing People, Not Just Properties

In the world of property management, it's not just about the buildings – it's about the people who call those buildings home. Dealing with all sorts of personalities is part of the gig for landlords. Sometimes, tenants see every little hiccup as a major crisis, and it's up to you to figure out what's truly urgent and what can wait. Being a good landlord means keeping your tenants happy while also keeping your own peace of mind intact. After all, your tenants aren't just customers – they're like your co-workers in this property adventure. Building a positive relationship with them is crucial for keeping them around and protecting your investment for the long haul.

Managing tenants isn't just about fixing leaky faucets or collecting rent – it's about understanding their needs and concerns. It's about being there when they need you, whether it's a busted pipe or a noisy neighbor situation. Communication is key in this landlord-tenant dance. Keeping the lines of communication open helps prevent misunderstandings and keeps everyone on the same page. When tenants feel heard and respected, they're more likely to stick around, which means fewer vacancies and a healthier bottom line for you.

Remember, being a landlord isn't just a business – it's a relationship. Building trust and rapport with your tenants can make all the difference in the world. So, while it may feel like a juggling act at times, finding that sweet spot between meeting your tenants' needs and looking out for your own interests is the secret sauce to successful property management.

Mastering property management procedures is an indispensable skill for real estate investors. By implementing structured and consistent processes, you can minimize risks, streamline operations, and enhance the overall experience for both yourself and your tenants. Understanding the importance of treating real estate as a business and managing the people within your properties will enable you to navigate the challenges of property management more effectively. As you refine your procedures and adapt them to your preferences, you will find greater control, peace, and success in your real estate investment journey. As you grow your number of properties, you'll then need to bring more staff on board. I talk more about this in chapter twelve.

Chapter Nine: Bookkeeping & Accounting

Before I continue, I want to make it clear that I am not a CPA or financial advisor, so do NOT take this as professional or legal financial advice. Accounting and bookkeeping play crucial roles in the successful management of rental properties, and it is important that you go in knowing a general overview of what to expect. As a landlord or property manager, it's essential to have a solid understanding of these financial processes to ensure accurate record-keeping, effective decision-making, and compliance with tax obligations. Let's delve into the key aspects of accounting and bookkeeping for landlords and property managers.

Accounting and bookkeeping provide a systematic approach to track income, expenses, and financial transactions related to your rental properties. By maintaining accurate records, you can monitor the financial health of your real estate investments, evaluate profitability, prepare tax returns, and make informed business decisions. Proper accounting also helps in documenting transactions for legal and regulatory purposes.

In the beginning things will be relatively easy for you since you will most likely be starting with a one- or two-family (duplex) property at the beginning of your investing journey. I am urging you to start with good habits early so that the transition to scale up to more units is easily attainable if that is your goal. If that's not your goal, that's okay too; you are the master of your destiny so you can be any size landlord you like as long as you are happy and satisfied with the life you are living.

Tenant Security Deposits

Whether you hold your rental properties under your personal name or a business entity, it is essential to maintain a separate bank account for rent collection and tenant security deposits. Implementing a systematic tracking system for rent receipts and payments is crucial. When a tenant moves in, it is customary to collect a security deposit from them. The specific amount may vary based on the tenant's credibility, but at a minimum, one month's rent is typically requested as security.

It is vital to deposit these funds into a distinct account separate from your other finances. This practice ensures compliance with state laws and prevents the mingling of funds. Commingling occurs when personal and non-personal funds are combined in the same account and misused for unintended purposes.

For instance, using a tenant's security deposit to pay personal credit card bills is both illegal and discouraged. In the unfortunate event that a tenant moves out and is owed a security deposit, failing to have the necessary funds readily available for refunding can lead to legal consequences and disfavor from judges. By adhering to these practices, you uphold legal compliance, safeguard tenant funds, and maintain ethical conduct as a landlord.

Recording Transactions

When it comes to managing the financial aspects of your rental properties, the first step involves documenting all sources of income and all expenses as well. This encompasses a spectrum of financial transactions, including rental income, security deposits, maintenance costs, repairs, property management fees, insurance premiums, property taxes, and mortgage payments.

By consistently tracking these financial elements, you gain a clear and transparent view of your rental properties' fiscal health. This comprehensive approach isn't just about paperwork; it serves as the foundation for effective financial management and informed decision-making in the realm of property ownership.

Chart of Accounts

Setting up a chart of accounts is like creating a personal map for your property finances. It's a categorized list of financial accounts, and for new landlords in property management, that might include things like Rental Income, Maintenance Expenses, Property Taxes, Insurance Costs, Mortgage Payments, and Property Management Fees. This organized approach is like having a financial toolkit, helping you navigate the money side of property management with ease.

Think of it as the GPS for your financial data, making it simpler to understand and analyze how your property's finances is going strong.

Bank Reconciliation

Regularly reconcile your bank statements with your recorded transactions to double-check to make sure everything adds up. Just compare your recorded transactions with the bank statement and tweak anything that looks off. This way, you catch any discrepancies early on and keep your property finances running smooth.

Financial Statements

Generate financial statements on a regular basis to gain insights into your property's financial health. The key financial statements for landlords and property managers are the Income Statement (also known as Profit and Loss Statement), Balance Sheet, and Cash Flow Statement. These statements provide a snapshot of your property's income, expenses, assets, liabilities, and cash flow.

Tracking Income and Expenses

Use accounting software or spreadsheets to track and categorize income and expenses. Accounting software such as QuickBooks, Xero, or FreshBooks can automate many tasks, streamline your bookkeeping process, and generate accurate financial reports. Spreadsheets like Microsoft Excel or Google Sheets can also be used effectively for basic bookkeeping.

Tax Compliance

Proper accounting and bookkeeping ensure that you maintain accurate records for tax purposes. You can easily calculate and report your rental income, deductible expenses, and depreciation to accurately complete your tax returns. Consult with a tax professional or accountant to ensure compliance with local tax regulations and maximize your tax benefits.

There is an often overlooked aspect of real estate investing that holds incredible power and benefits: the ability to use real estate ownership to offset and reduce tax liabilities. Once you grasp this concept, you'll realize that the real game we're playing is not a rat race, but rather a tax game. To win this game, you need to maximize your income and minimize your tax payments, and real estate ownership can help you achieve that. While I won't delve into the intricacies in this book, I encourage you to research and educate yourself on this topic when you have the time.

When the year comes to an end, you'll need to meet with your CPA or tax preparer to provide them with a comprehensive breakdown of your income and expenses. If you've followed my advice and diligently tracked all your financial transactions, this process should be smooth and straightforward. By staying organized and providing detailed records, you'll minimize the need for extensive questioning. As you gain experience over the first year or so, you'll become adept at this process, and it will transform into an enjoyable game of finding ways to increase cash flow and reduce expenses.

Chapter Ten: Legal Issues and Evictions

Hopefully, you won't need to refer to this chapter frequently, but unfortunately, legal issues and evictions are part of the business, and most experienced landlords have encountered them at some point in their career. Ideally, these situations would arise at least three years into your investing journey. Let's delve into some of the common legal issues you may face as a landlord and explore them one by one, as you may be unfamiliar with the terminology.

Landlord Tenant Laws

Landlord-tenant laws are a set of legal regulations that govern the rights and responsibilities of both landlords and tenants in a rental housing arrangement. These laws vary by jurisdiction, as they are typically established at the state or local level. Understanding landlord-tenant laws is essential for you to ensure compliance, maintain healthy tenant relationships, and protect your interests. As long as you're doing what you're supposed to do, you won't have to worry about tenants trying to take legal action against you. Here are some key aspects of landlord-tenant laws:

Lease Agreements

Landlord-tenant laws require lease agreements to be legally enforceable contracts. They outline the terms and conditions of the tenancy, including rent amount, payment schedule, lease duration, and tenant obligations. Landlords may be required to provide specific information to tenants, such as lead-based paint disclosures, notice of any known hazards, or rights to privacy. Certain lease provisions may be deemed illegal or unenforceable under landlord-tenant laws. Examples include clauses that waive tenants' rights or impose excessive financial penalties.

Rent and Security Deposits

In some areas, local regulations may limit how much a landlord can increase rent and provide guidelines for rent stabilization. This is called rent control. Laws typically regulate the collection, storage, and return of security deposits. They may impose limits on the amount that can be collected and specify the time frame for returning the deposit or providing an itemized deduction statement. Rent is the biggest legal issue that landlords face.

Habitability and Maintenance

Landlords are generally required to provide safe and habitable living conditions for tenants. This includes ensuring adequate heating, plumbing, electricity, and addressing structural issues or pest infestations. This is called Implied Warranty of Habitability. Landlords may have legal obligations to promptly address repair requests that affect the habitability of the rental unit. Failure to do so may allow tenants certain remedies, such as rent withholding or lease termination.

Tenant Privacy and Entry

Landlords must adhere to specific rules regarding entry into a tenant's rental unit. These laws typically require advance notice, often 24 to 48 hours, except in emergencies or other specific circumstances. This is called Notice of Entry. Tenant privacy is protected under landlord-tenant laws, prohibiting landlords from entering the rental unit without proper notice or without a legitimate reason. These are called Privacy Rights.

Evictions

Some jurisdictions have "just cause" eviction laws, which restrict landlords from evicting tenants without a valid reason, such as non-payment of rent, lease violations, or property damage. These are called Just Cause Evictions. Landlord-tenant laws outline the legal process for eviction, including providing written notices, filing eviction lawsuits, attending court hearings, and executing eviction orders. Specific time frames and procedures vary by jurisdiction.

Anti-Discrimination Laws

Federal and state fair housing laws prohibit landlords from discriminating against tenants based on protected characteristics such as race, color, religion, national origin, sex, disability, and familial status. Additional protected classes may exist at the local level. These are called Fair Housing Laws.

It's important to note that landlord-tenant laws can be complex and subject to change. It is advisable to consult with a local attorney or a professional familiar with the specific laws in your jurisdiction to ensure compliance and to address any legal questions or concerns.

Landlord vs Tenant Issues

These are three of the most common tenant issues that you may encounter during your time as a landlord, but don't worry, I got you covered. As someone who has experienced and successfully navigated these situations, you have your own personal step-by-step playbook.

Non-payment of rent refers to a situation where a tenant, who is either on a current lease or has transitioned to a month-to-month tenancy after the lease expiration, fails to pay their rent or other charges that can be considered as rent. For instance, if a tenant is responsible for a portion of the water bill in a rented house or townhouse, or if the property has sub-metering to bill each tenant individually, the amount owed for water can be classified as a rent charge. In such cases, landlords have the legal right to take action against non-payment, similar to when a tenant fails to pay their actual rent. This action may include initiating eviction proceedings. However, it is advisable not to resort to eviction threats immediately. Eviction should be considered as a last resort, as pursuing this course of action can involve court or legal fees.

If you find yourself in a situation where a tenant has not paid their rent, it is important to establish rapport and open lines of communication with the tenant. While it may be easier with some tenants than others, it is worth trying to understand their circumstances and see if there is a feasible solution to resolve the issue. If verbal communication proves ineffective, it is recommended to progress to written communication, clearly outlining deadlines for payment. The specific rules around timelines and notices can vary from state to state, so it is essential to check with local municipalities to ensure compliance with the law. The workbook supplementing this book provides an example of what such a letter may look like. If written communication and open dialogue fail to yield results, it may be necessary to set firm deadlines, such as specifying a dollar amount (e.g., if the tenant owes more than $500), and consider initiating legal proceedings. Many tenants would prefer to avoid a court case or a judgment against them, prompting them to either start making payments or communicate their plans to catch up on the overdue rent.

When a tenant does not move out when their lease ends, it is typically referred to as a "holdover tenancy" or "tenancy at sufferance." In this situation, the tenant continues to occupy the rental property without the landlord's permission or a valid lease agreement in place. *Holdover tenancy* occurs when the tenant remains in the property beyond the lease term without renewing the lease or reaching a new agreement with the landlord. The tenant is essentially "holding over" and is no longer entitled to the same rights and protections provided by the original lease.

When dealing with a holdover tenancy as a landlord, the process typically involves reviewing the lease agreement to confirm the expiration date and any provisions related to holdover tenancy. Then, communicate with the tenant to remind them that their lease has expired and request that they vacate the premises promptly. It's advisable to have these communications in writing to create a paper trail.

Depending on the circumstances, you may choose to offer the tenant a new lease or renewal agreement. If the tenant does not respond or refuses to vacate, serve them with a legal notice to quit, formally demanding that they surrender possession of the property within a specified period.

If the tenant still fails to vacate the property after receiving the notice to quit, you may need to initiate an eviction lawsuit. This involves filing a complaint or petition with the appropriate court to obtain a legal judgment for possession of the property. Attend the scheduled eviction hearing to present your case before a judge. The tenant will also have an opportunity to present their defense. If the judge rules in your favor, an order of possession will be issued, granting you the right to regain control of the property.

If the tenant continues to resist or refuses to vacate, you may need to involve law enforcement or hire a professional eviction service to physically remove the tenant from the property. The specifics of enforcement can vary depending on local laws and procedures.

Throughout the process, it's crucial to consult with an attorney or seek legal advice to ensure compliance with local laws and regulations. Eviction laws and procedures can vary significantly depending on the jurisdiction, so it's important to follow the appropriate legal steps to protect your rights as a landlord.

Another issue that may occur is when a renter illegally rents out your property to someone else without your knowledge or permission. It is commonly referred to as "illegal use of property," "subletting without authorization," or "unauthorized subletting."

If you discover illegal use of the property or unauthorized subletting by a tenant, review the lease agreement to determine if it prohibits subletting or specifies approved uses of the property. Gather evidence to support your claim, such as photographs or witness statements.

As always, initiate a conversation with the tenant to discuss the issue and seek an explanation, maintaining open communication throughout the process.

If the lease agreement prohibits the specific activity, you have to issue a formal notice to the tenant, outlining the violation and required actions. The notice may include a deadline for the tenant to cease the illegal activity or terminate the unauthorized subletting.

Depending on the severity of the violation, you may offer potential resolutions such as terminating the unauthorized subletting or revising the lease agreement. Alternatively, if the tenant fails to comply with the notice, you can pursue legal action by filing an eviction lawsuit or seeking a court order to regain possession of the property.

Throughout the process, I highly recommend that you consult with legal professionals to ensure compliance with local laws and regulations and receive guidance on the best course of action.

It's important to familiarize yourself with applicable landlord-tenant laws and seek legal advice when necessary to handle the situation appropriately and protect their rights.

Chapter Eleven: Section 8 and Other Agency Housing Programs

In this chapter, we will explore the benefits and processes of renting properties to government agencies such as Section 8, veterans programs, mental health programs, and other social service programs. These housing programs can provide a steady stream of income and offer reassurance to landlords. While we will primarily focus on Section 8, the principles discussed can be applied to other housing programs as well. This chapter aims to provide you with insights and strategies to leverage these programs effectively. This is where the money resides!

Partnering with Government Agencies

Renting properties to government agencies can create a safety net for landlords, ensuring a consistent flow of rents. It is recommended that new investors, whether operating locally or remotely, consider partnering with these agencies. By doing so, you can have confidence in receiving a significant portion of your rents. While dealing with these agencies may involve some challenges and administrative tasks, the long-term benefits outweigh the initial hurdles. Agencies such as Section 8, veterans programs, and mental health programs can be instrumental in building a successful real estate portfolio.

Understanding Section 8

Section 8 is a prominent housing program that has helped numerous landlords achieve substantial financial growth. This section will delve into the specifics of Section 8 and offer practical insights based on personal experiences. However, it is important to note that each local Housing Authority may have specific guidelines and procedures, so it is advisable to contact your local authority for detailed information.

To summarize, Section 8 housing refers to a federal housing assistance program established by the United States Department of Housing and Urban Development (HUD). It is officially known as the Housing Choice Voucher Program. Section 8 aims to provide safe and affordable housing options to low-income individuals, families, the elderly, and disabled persons.

Under the Section 8 program, eligible participants receive rental assistance vouchers that subsidize a portion of their monthly rent. These vouchers are issued by local public housing agencies (PHAs) and can be used by tenants to rent housing from private landlords who participate in the program.

The amount of rental assistance provided through Section 8 is based on the tenant's income, family size, and the local rental market. The program sets a payment standard, which is the maximum amount the housing agency will subsidize, and the tenant is responsible for paying the difference between the actual rent and the subsidy amount. The payment standard is typically set at a percentage of the area's median income.

Landlords who choose to participate in the Section 8 program agree to abide by certain rules and regulations. They must meet HUD's housing quality standards, ensuring that the rental units are safe, sanitary, and in good condition. The rent charged by landlords must also be reasonable and within the limits established by the program.

Section 8 provides benefits to both tenants and landlords. For tenants, it offers access to affordable housing in the private rental market, allowing them to choose suitable housing for their needs. Landlords benefit by receiving guaranteed rental payments from the housing agency, reducing the risk of rent defaults.

Overall, Section 8 plays a crucial role in addressing housing affordability issues and providing support to low-income individuals and families in securing decent and affordable housing.

To begin, it is recommended to approach the Section 8 rental process with a clear understanding of your desired outcome. Researching the HUD website will provide valuable information about maximum allowable rents in your area based on property type and location. Utilizing online platforms such as AffordableHousing.com to list your properties can attract potential tenants. Taking appealing pictures and setting a reasonable asking rent are crucial factors in generating interest. If needed, exploring alternative platforms like Facebook or Craigslist can also be effective.

Open House and Application Review

Once you start receiving inquiries, scheduling an open house allows prospective tenants to view the property. It is important to treat all applicants equally and avoid any discriminatory practices. Some applicants may have vouchers (Agency Subsidy), while others may be market-rate tenants qualifying based on their income. A phone script provided in the accompanying handbook can serve as a useful reference during your interactions with potential tenants. After the open house, reviewing the applications and conducting thorough screenings will help you select the most suitable tenant for your property. Sample application forms included in the handbook can assist in streamlining this process.

Renting to Voucher Holders

A housing voucher, also known as a rental assistance voucher, is a document provided to eligible individuals or families participating in housing assistance programs such as the Section 8 Housing Choice Voucher Program. The voucher is issued by a local public housing agency (PHA) and serves as a subsidy that helps the recipient pay for housing in the private rental market.

The purpose of a housing voucher is to bridge the gap between the recipient's income and the cost of rental housing. The voucher represents a specific amount of financial assistance that can be used towards monthly rental payments. The exact value of the voucher is determined based on factors such as the recipient's income, family size, and the local rental market conditions.

Once a recipient receives a housing voucher, they can search for a rental unit in the private market that meets their needs and is within the program's guidelines. The voucher holder typically has the freedom to choose any rental property that meets the program's requirements, including location, size, and condition.

When the voucher holder finds a suitable rental unit, they enter into a lease agreement with the landlord. The voucher holder is responsible for paying a portion of the rent directly to the landlord, typically based on their income, while the housing voucher covers the remaining portion.

The housing voucher program provides benefits to both tenants and landlords. For tenants, it offers the opportunity to secure safe and affordable housing that may not have been otherwise attainable. Landlords benefit by receiving guaranteed rental payments from the housing agency, reducing the risk of rent defaults.

It's important to note that housing voucher programs have specific rules and regulations that participants must follow. These may include requirements regarding income eligibility, lease agreements, and housing quality standards. Each program may have its own guidelines, so it's essential for voucher recipients and landlords to understand and adhere to the specific rules of their program.

If you decide to rent to a tenant with a voucher, you will need to complete a packet provided by the housing authority. This initiates the process, and once both you and the prospective tenant have completed the packet, it is submitted to the housing authority. Subsequently, a property inspection will be scheduled to ensure the property meets the necessary safety standards. The handbook includes a template with a list of items inspectors typically check during the inspection. In the event that the property does not pass inspection initially, the inspector will provide guidance on the necessary improvements for a re-inspection. Upon successfully passing the inspection, you will receive an official move-in letter from the housing authority, outlining the payment breakdown between the authority and the tenant.

Renting properties through Section 8 and other housing programs can be a lucrative venture for landlords. While the process may involve some initial effort and adherence to program guidelines, the rewards are significant. By leveraging these programs, landlords can enjoy a consistent flow of income and establish long-term financial stability. It is essential to stay proactive and prepared for any maintenance issues that may arise. With the right approach and knowledge, Section 8 and other housing programs can be a valuable asset in your real estate investment journey.

Chapter Twelve: Staffing For Your Rental Properties

Deciding whether to hire a property manager or create your own team is a personal choice that depends on your circumstances. However, I generally recommend starting off by managing your property yourself, first. This allows you to familiarize yourself with the responsibilities of a property manager and gain firsthand experience. The duration of time you choose to manage the property on your own is entirely up to you. It's crucial to take your time and carefully select the right individuals if you decide to outsource the management tasks to a team or if you prefer to build and expand your own team.

I have personally experienced both approaches, and each has its own set of challenges. Here are some pros and cons to consider:

Pros of Hiring Staffers:
- Having staffers can save you significant time and effort by delegating various tasks.
- Hiring professionals with expertise in property management can bring valuable knowledge and experience to the table.
- As your rental property portfolio grows, having a team of staffers enables you to scale your operations more efficiently.
- With a team in place, you may be able to provide additional services to your tenants.

Cons of Hiring Staffers:
- Hiring staffers comes with financial implications. You'll need to consider salaries, benefits, payroll taxes, and potentially additional expenses.
- Recruiting and retaining reliable and competent staff members can be challenging.
- When you have staffers handling various aspects of property management, you may feel a loss of control over certain decisions and operations.
- Relying on staffers means that your business is dependent on their performance and availability.

Ultimately, the decision to hire staffers for your rental properties depends on factors such as the size of your portfolio, your availability, your budget, and your comfort level with delegating responsibilities.

It's important to weigh the pros and cons, assess your specific needs, and carefully consider the potential impact on your business before making a decision.

Of course, the next question is always, "how do I know when I'm ready to add staff to my rentals?" I can't answer that for you. Determining when it's time to add staff to your rental properties is a personal decision influenced by various factors. Here are some indications that you may be ready to expand your team:

Portfolio Size
If your property portfolio is growing, managing numerous properties on your own can become overwhelming. The increasing workload may suggest that it's time to consider hiring staff.

Time Constraints
If property management tasks are consuming a significant portion of your time, leaving little room for other important aspects of your life or business, it could be a sign that delegating some responsibilities to staff would be beneficial.

Expertise and Specialized Needs
As your rental property business evolves, you may encounter tasks that require specific knowledge or expertise. If you find yourself lacking the necessary skills or struggling with complex management aspects, hiring staff with the right expertise can be advantageous.

Financial Considerations
Assess your financial situation to determine if you have the resources to hire and sustain staff. Consider the potential return on investment and weigh the benefits of adding staff against the associated costs.

Desire for Growth and Expansion
If you have ambitious goals to grow your rental property business and venture into new areas, having a team in place can provide the support needed to achieve those goals more efficiently.

Personal Capacity and Well-Being
Reflect on your personal well-being and work-life balance. If managing properties on your own is causing excessive stress, negatively impacting your health, or depriving you of personal time, it may be an indication that adding staff could alleviate the burden.

If you found yourself saying yes to a good number of these, then great! If you can afford it, then you should reward it. When it comes to property management, having a reliable and capable team is paramount to success. Be prepared though, the process of hiring staff requires careful planning and execution.

Define Roles and Responsibilities

First, figure out who's doing what. For example, if you're hiring a property manager, think about what they'll be handling — day-to-day operations, keeping tenants happy, making sure everything's up to code. Now, a leasing agent? They're the ones spreading the word about vacant spots, showing folks around, and sealing the deal on leases. Be clear on these responsibilities so everyone knows their role and what they are expected to deliver.

Next up, what skills are you looking for? Maybe your property manager needs to be a smooth talker and a problem-solver. Maintenance staff should know their way around a toolbox. Also, think about how each role fits into the team—property management is a team sport. Check if the roles complement each other, fostering an environment where everyone works together smoothly.

Lastly, think ahead. Where do you see your property management crew in a couple of years? Make roles adaptable to changes and consider growth opportunities for your team. Also, find folks whose values click with your company culture. Don't forget about flexibility—sometimes, roles need to wear a few different hats, especially in a smaller team. Finally, create a budget for either a salary or competitive hourly rate for the role so that you won't have high turnover rates with staff. This sets you up for a solid, future-proof property management team.

Now, you're ready to get some qualified applicants.

Utilize Online Job Platforms and Network in the Industry

Take advantage of online job platforms such as LinkedIn, Indeed, or specialized real estate job boards to post your openings. LinkedIn offers unparalleled professional networking, Indeed is a go-to with a vast candidate pool, and specialized real estate job boards cater specifically to property professionals. Post your openings on these platforms to broaden your reach and tap into diverse talent pools.

Once you create your accounts on whatever platforms you choose, take the time to make your job listings stand out. Clearly outline what you're looking for and showcase what makes your property management team exceptional. Highlight perks, whether it's a vibrant work culture, growth opportunities, or unique projects. Your listing should not just seek candidates; it should entice them to be part of your team. Do not just post the job, but engage actively on these platforms. Join relevant groups and forums, participate in discussions, and demonstrate the uniqueness of your property management team. It's not just about finding talent; it's about showcasing why potential candidates should choose your property over others.

Extend your reach by leveraging social media platforms. Share job listings on Instagram and Facebook. Social media is your megaphone, amplifying your message to a broader audience. Additionally, consider attending virtual networking events and industry-specific gatherings. Leverage your industry connections and networks to find suitable candidates; remember, personal referrals can often lead to exceptional hires. Connect with potential candidates and let them see the personality behind your property management team.

This goes without saying, but ensure your company website serves as a welcoming gateway. Make your careers page easily accessible, showcasing what makes joining your property management team a compelling opportunity. Your website often acts as the first touchpoint for interested candidates, so make it count. Get online, stand out, and build the dream team you envision.

Review Resumes and Applications

Screen resumes and applications to shortlist candidates whose qualifications align with your requirements. Look for relevant experience and skills in property management, as well as a track record of success. You're going to want to create a shortlist of the top 15 candidates, then conduct initial interviews to assess candidates' communication skills, cultural fit, and general suitability for the role. Use this stage to gauge their enthusiasm and understanding of property management principles. A good additional tip is to implement a skills assessments or practical exercises to evaluate candidates' abilities in key areas like customer service, problem-solving, and proficiency with property management software. This step provides valuable insights into their practical skills.

At this point you should have been able to eliminate at least half of your list based on interviews alone. Now, you're going to whittle your list down to the top 10. It's going to be difficult, but one way to make it easier is to contact the references provided by candidates to verify their work history, performance, and reliability. This step is helps gather insights from previous employers or colleagues about a candidate's strengths and areas for development, plus it helps you suss out any red flags that candidates may have.

Conduct Second Round of Interviews

For top candidates, conduct a second round of interviews. Dive deeper into their experience by asking about specific accomplishments and how they handled challenges in previous roles. Assess their problem-solving skills with relevant scenarios, shedding light on their analytical abilities.

Cultural fit is equally important. Understand their values, work style, and collaboration approach to ensure harmony within your property management team. Evaluate their adaptability to industry dynamics by exploring instances where they've navigated change. Gauge long-term commitment by discussing career goals, seeking candidates envisioning growth within your organization.

Consider involving key team members in this round for diverse perspectives. Be transparent about role expectations and potential challenges, providing candidates with a clear understanding. Showcase your property management team's culture, sharing success stories and emphasizing collaboration.

The second round is about finding not just the right skills but the perfect fit — someone aligned with your company culture and committed to the long-term success of your property management team. Dive in, ask the essential questions, and build that dream team. This is also the time to openly talk about the compensation package, benefits, and any other relevant details during the final stages of the hiring process. Transparency is key to managing expectations and building trust with potential team members.

Extend Job Offers and Onboarding

Once you've found the right person, it's time to lock in that perfect addition to your property management team. When extending a job offer, keep it clear and transparent. Outline the nitty-gritty details— salary, benefits, and perks. Be upfront about expectations, discussing the role thoroughly to avoid any surprises later. Negotiate with flexibility, recognizing that candidates might have specific needs. Give them time to mull it over; decisions like these need careful consideration. Express genuine enthusiasm about having them on board, and promptly follow up to answer any questions.

Once they accept, formalize the offer with a written agreement. Discuss the onboarding plan, ensuring a smooth transition into the team. And don't forget to celebrate the new hire — whether it's a welcome message or a shout-out during team meetings. Extending a job offer isn't just about filling a position; it's the start of a collaborative journey with your property management family.

Continuous Training and Development

After assembling your dream team, the next chapter is all about continuous training.

Stay ahead in property management by keeping your team updated on industry trends and advancements. Encourage professional growth through workshops, seminars, and online courses, fostering a team that stays ahead of the game.

Embrace versatility with cross-training, making your team adaptable to various aspects of property management. Ensure they're tech-savvy by keeping them well-versed in the latest software and digital tools. Foster a culture of continuous learning through collaborative sessions and regular team meetings. Tailor training to individual goals, cultivate leadership qualities, and continuously assess and adapt your training strategies based on team feedback. This way, you're not just maintaining excellence; you're propelling your property management team toward ongoing success.

By following these steps and investing time in the hiring process, you can assemble a team that not only possesses the necessary skills but also aligns with your company values and goals. Building a solid property management team sets the stage for long-term success in the industry as a long distance landlord. Get it done!

Chapter Thirteen: Next Steps

Despite the tough decisions and challenges that you may have faced, you've reached this point in the book and the real-life process already. That automatically makes you a success! I hope you consider this book as a valuable resource that you can refer back to throughout your investing journey. I also created a workbook to assist you when you encounter obstacles along the way. From personal experience, I know how challenging it can be to find the right form or letter when you need it. Register on the website LongDistanceMillionaire.com and you will receive updates to the workbook as policies evolve and expand, ensuring that it grows with your business.

If you feel like you've only scratched the surface and require further assistance in embarking on your journey as a landlord, I would like to extend an invitation to join my Step-by-Step Academy. This program offers comprehensive, one-on-one mentorship with myself and the SBS Community to exponentially increase your success in closing on a property.

By joining the Step-by-Step Academy, you're taking a significant step towards realizing your dreams of becoming a successful real estate investor. With personalized mentorship, access to a supportive community, and a comprehensive curriculum, you'll have the tools and guidance necessary to close on your first property with confidence. Don't miss out on this exclusive opportunity to accelerate your journey to success. Visit www.SBSAcademy.us today to learn more and secure your spot in the academy.

The Step-by-Step Academy (SBS Academy) is a comprehensive learning academy to that will teach you investing strategies such as real estate investing, wealth building strategies, stock investing, business building, retirement strategies, advanced wealth management through insurance, generational money management, and so much more. It provides you with not only a community, but a one-on-one mentorship component that is available if you need more hand holding. The mentorship options are self-paced mentorship, 90-day mentorship, and lifetime mentorship.

By breaking down daunting investing objectives into smaller manageable steps, your probability greatly increases of accomplishing your goals in less time than you can imagine. We offer you the ability to create a customized and curated program that is tailored to your specific needs, circumstances, and goals so that we can meet you where you are and get you where you want to be. What's even better is that you don't have to go at it alone.

The SBS Academy members are absolutely amazing! It is truly a place where you get the opportunity to build real relationships. Everyone can learn from everyone else, and most importantly, everyone has something that they can teach everyone else. Once you are a member of the SBS Academy you will have access to the private Facebook group, the VIP Telegram group, ongoing VIP investing strategies, monthly SBS newsletter, and investment opportunities exclusively available to SBS members.

The right mentorship can be an incredibly valuable asset. Learning from an experienced mentor that has real life experience can shave years off the learning curve and help you reach success so much faster. I have students that were trying to figure out the matrix of investing on their own for four or five years and within 3 months of joining the SBS Academy they accomplished a monumental goal of closing on their first investment property! They attribute this success solely to the SBS Academy mentorship. Some of them were excited to share their experiences in their own words. See some of the testimonials below:

> "Working with Andre Green has been an impactful experience. The opportunity to receive his assistance has helped me reposition and realigned me with my financial goals. He thoroughly communicates the details of the process while also guiding me to success over the course of the journey. I have received more advice than I actually am able to compensate him for. I would strongly recommend that someone use his services because he is knowledgeable on the subject matter and surpasses all of the other people I went to see before him."
>
> - Ola Aiyedun

"If you're struggling to make progress in real estate or need that extra push to achieve your goals, I wholeheartedly recommend Andre Green and his Step-by-Step Academy. With his personalized mentorship and proven methods, you'll gain the confidence, knowledge, and strategies needed to succeed. I'm grateful to have found Andre, and I can't wait to see what the future holds for my real estate endeavors."

- Goran Mrvic

"I have worked with Andre to secure insurance for my home, business credit for my new business and receive advice on real estate and property management more broadly. With each subject, Andre manages to boil down complex analyses from his breadth of knowledge and convey them in relatable terms. This has made conversations about investments and returns that are typically intimidating, feel like I am talking to a friend who is invested in me "getting it";. Such moments have been the difference in me feeling like I am capable of taking control of my financial future in a transformative way. It's clear Andre is in business wanting many to win, investing his time in podcasts, panels and other educational outlets to share the valuable information he has."

- Michelle Mondesir

"I had the honor of being mentored by Andre Green for the past two years. I was in the midst of buying a family property and because of him, I am thriving as a multi-family homeowner. He took a complicated and personal matter and made sure I was able to navigate it with ease. He shared loan options, insurance options, and legal options to complete the final sale. I am so grateful for the wealth of knowledge he shared, but his guidance, support, and ingenuity makes him one of a kind in this industry. I would not be where I am today without him."

- Zenia Duran

By joining the Step-by-Step Academy, you're taking a significant step towards realizing your dreams of becoming a successful real estate investor. With personalized mentorship, access to a supportive community, and a comprehensive curriculum, you'll have the tools and guidance necessary to close on your first property with confidence. Don't miss out on this exclusive opportunity to accelerate your journey to success. Visit www.SBSAcademy.us today to learn more and secure your spot in the academy. You can choose which SBS Academy program best suits your lifestyle by visiting the website and clicking "Join SBS Academy." Follow the prompts to start learning.

I sincerely hope that this book brings you prosperity, knowledge, and good fortune on your path to becoming a millionaire! I would love to hear your success stories, so please share them with me. See you at the top of the mountain!

Glossary

Amortization: Amortization refers to the gradual repayment of a loan or mortgage through regular payments over a specific period. It includes both principal and interest payments, with a larger portion going towards interest at the beginning of the loan term.

Appraisal: An appraisal is an unbiased assessment of a property's value conducted by a qualified appraiser. It determines the fair market value based on various factors such as location, condition, comparable properties, and market trends.

Buyer's Market: A buyer's market occurs when there are more properties for sale than potential buyers. This situation often results in decreased property prices, longer days on the market, and increased negotiating power for buyers.

Capital Gains: Capital gains are the profits realized from the sale of a property or investment. It represents the difference between the selling price and the original purchase price. Capital gains may be subject to taxes.

Capitalization Rate (Cap Rate): The capitalization rate is a measure used to assess the potential return on investment for an income-producing property. It is calculated by dividing the property's net operating income (NOI) by its purchase price or current market value. A higher cap rate indicates a higher potential return.

Closing Costs: Closing costs are expenses incurred by the buyer and seller during the property purchase transaction. These costs include fees for title searches, inspections, appraisals, loan origination, attorney fees, and taxes. They are typically paid at the closing of the sale.

Comparative Market Analysis (CMA): A comparative market analysis is an evaluation of similar properties in the same area that helps determine a property's market value. It assists in setting an appropriate listing price or making an offer to purchase.

Contingency: A contingency is a condition or requirement that must be met for a real estate transaction to proceed. Common contingencies include inspections, financing, and the sale of the buyer's existing property.

Conveyance: Conveyance is the legal process of transferring ownership of a property from one party to another. It involves the preparation and execution of necessary documents, such as deeds and transfer forms.

Depreciation: Depreciation is the decrease in value of a property over time due to factors such as wear and tear, obsolescence, or aging. It is commonly used for tax purposes, allowing property owners to deduct a portion of the property's value as an expense.

Down Payment: The down payment is the initial upfront payment made by the buyer when purchasing a property. It is a percentage of the total purchase price and is typically paid in cash or through financing.

Earnest Money Deposit (EMD): Earnest money, also known as a good faith deposit, is a sum of money provided by the buyer as a demonstration of their serious intent to purchase a property. It is typically held in escrow and applied towards the down payment or closing costs.

Escrow: Escrow is a process in which a neutral third party holds funds, documents, or assets on behalf of the buyer and seller during a real estate transaction. The escrow agent ensures that all conditions and obligations are met before releasing the funds or transferring the property title.

Equity: Equity refers to the ownership interest or value that an owner has in a property after subtracting any outstanding debts or liens. It represents the difference between the property's market value and the amount owed on mortgages or loans.

Eviction: Eviction is the legal process of removing a tenant from a rental property due to violations of the lease agreement, non-payment of rent, or other valid reasons specified by local landlord-tenant laws.

Fair Housing Act: The Fair Housing Act is a federal law in the United States that prohibits discrimination in housing based on race, color, religion, sex, national origin, disability, and familial status. Landlords must comply with these anti-discrimination laws when selecting tenants and enforcing rental policies.

Home Inspection: A home inspection is a thorough examination of a property's condition conducted by a professional inspector. It assesses the structural integrity, systems, and components of the property to identify any issues or potential problems.

Homeowners Association (HOA): A homeowners association is an organization that manages and maintains common areas and amenities within a community or condominium complex. Members of the association pay regular fees and adhere to specific rules and regulations.

Landlord Insurance: Landlord insurance is a specific type of property insurance that provides coverage for rental properties. It typically includes property damage, liability protection, and loss of rental income in case of damage or unforeseen circumstances.

Landlord-Tenant Law: Landlord-tenant law refers to the legal framework that governs the rights and obligations of landlords and tenants. It includes regulations related to lease agreements, eviction processes, security deposits, fair housing practices, and other aspects of the landlord-tenant relationship.

Lease Option: A lease option, also known as a rent-to-own agreement, is a contract that allows a tenant to lease a property with the option to purchase it at a later date. It gives the tenant the opportunity to test the property before committing to the purchase.

Lease Renewal: Lease renewal refers to the process of extending the existing lease agreement with a current tenant for an additional term. It involves renegotiating lease terms, including rent amount, lease duration, and any updated conditions.

Lease Term: Lease term refers to the duration or length of time for which a tenant agrees to rent a property. It is typically specified in the lease agreement and can range from a few months to several years.

Letter Of Intent (LOI): A non-binding document that outlines to a seller what your intentions are in purchasing a property and what your offer is.

Maintenance and Repairs: Landlords are responsible for maintaining the rental property and ensuring that it is in a habitable condition. This includes regular repairs, addressing maintenance issues, and providing essential services such as heating, plumbing, and electricity.

Mortgage: A mortgage is a loan provided by a lender to finance the purchase of a property. It is secured by the property itself, and the borrower makes regular payments (including principal and interest) over a specified period until the loan is fully repaid.

Occupancy Rate: Occupancy rate refers to the percentage of rented units or properties in a landlord's portfolio that are currently occupied by tenants. It is a measure of how well a landlord is able to keep their properties filled.

Property Management: Property management involves the day-to-day operations, maintenance, and oversight of rental properties on behalf of the landlord. It includes tasks such as rent collection, tenant communication, property maintenance, and handling legal and administrative responsibilities.

Rent Collection: Rent collection refers to the process of collecting rental payments from tenants. It can be done through various methods such as in-person payments, online payments, or automatic deductions.

Rental Application: A rental application is a form that prospective tenants complete to provide information about themselves, their employment, rental history, and other relevant details. Landlords use this information to screen and evaluate potential tenants.

Rental Property Analysis: Rental property analysis involves assessing the value and potential of a property for investment purposes. It includes analyzing factors such as location, market conditions, rental income potential, expenses, and return on investment.

Rental Property Management: Rental property management refers to the tasks and responsibilities involved in overseeing and operating rental properties. It includes tasks such as marketing and advertising vacancies, tenant screening, rent collection, property maintenance, and handling tenant concerns.

Rental Agreement/Lease: A rental agreement or lease is a legally binding contract between a landlord and a tenant that outlines the terms and conditions of the rental arrangement, such as rent amount, duration of tenancy, and rules and responsibilities of both parties.

Rental Income: Rental income refers to the money received by the landlord from tenants as payment for occupying the rental property. It is a primary source of revenue for landlords and contributes to the financial viability of the investment.

Rental Yield: Rental yield is a measure of the return on investment for a rental property. It is calculated by dividing the annual rental income by the property's purchase price or market value and expressing it as a percentage.

Security Deposit: A security deposit is a refundable amount of money paid by the tenant to the landlord at the beginning of the tenancy. It serves as protection for the landlord against any damages or unpaid rent caused by the tenant.

Seller's Market: A seller's market occurs when there are more buyers than available properties for sale. This situation often leads to increased property prices, multiple offers, and a competitive environment that favors sellers.

Tenant Screening: Tenant screening is the process of evaluating prospective tenants to assess their suitability as renters. It may involve checking credit history, conducting background checks, verifying income, and contacting references to make informed tenant selection decisions.

Tenant Turnover: Tenant turnover refers to the process of tenants moving out of a rental property and new tenants moving in. It includes tasks such as cleaning and preparing the unit for the next tenant, advertising vacancies, and screening and selecting new tenants.

Title: Title refers to the legal ownership rights and interests to a property. It confirms the lawful possession and control of the property by the owner. A title search is conducted to verify the property's ownership history, ensure there are no liens or claims against it, and issue title insurance to protect the buyer against any unforeseen issues.

Title Insurance: Title insurance is a type of insurance that protects the buyer and lender against any defects, liens, or disputes regarding the property's title. It provides financial coverage and legal support in case of unforeseen title-related issues.

Zoning: Zoning refers to the local government's regulations and restrictions on land use within specific areas or zones. It defines how the land can be used for residential, commercial, industrial, or other purposes, as well as restrictions on building height, density, setbacks, and other factors.

Index

R

S

T

U